Contents

Dedication

Dedicated to
Mohamed, Dounia & Daniya.

In loving memory of Kubrick,
charming feline, beloved friend,
occasional nuisance.

Acknowledgments

During the process of writing this book, whenever I would tell someone about it, I was usually met with very enthusiastic storytellers eager to share their cat story with me. Of course, I couldn't use them all, but I do thank everyone who at least tried. Your cats are still amazing, even if only to you. But a special word of gratitude goes out to those who contributed stories—often emailing me whatever headline they came across by accident—that ended up in the book. Those people are Nahreman Issa, Deborah Couch, Karen Payne, my parents Ahmed and Tamam, Kirstin Keppler and her abundant research on pet therapy, Faye Boer (who gets a bonus thanks for publishing this book), the many organizations that helped me find contacts and, of course, the small but generous contribution from Prime Minister Stephen Harper.

And I thank all my friends who spread the word about my cat book, making it especially difficult for me to have a non-cat-related conversation with new people. Thanks a lot guys.

Introduction

BEFORE READING *AMAZING CATS*, take a moment to look at your cat and search for the similarities between the two of you. The fact that you are reading this book means you are probably a cat lover, and it's very likely that your pet is snuggled up in your lap right now. So close this book and put it away for a moment (don't worry, unlike your cat, this book won't scurry away disinterested). Now concentrate on your kitty.

Are you back? What did you notice? You probably recognized a lot of unique differences and a few obvious similarities: ears, tongue, limbs and eyes. But look again at the eyes as they glow in the darkness or glaze in the light of your room. Biologically, cats have eyes very different from ours, but notice where they are. Like us, cats have eyes at the front of their heads, because, like us, they too are hunters.

Homo sapiens and *Felis silvestris catus* evolved from a common ancestor that lived about 200 million years ago. Whatever this creature was, it cautiously tiptoed through the dangers of the dinosaur dynasty. When an asteroid snuffed out the giant predators 65 million years ago, our ancestor was allowed to thrive and branch out into many more species. One developed tool-making and -shaping opposable thumbs, and another developed the meat cutting canines and tree-climbing claws. The latter became the cat. It and its relatives were a successful bunch that populated every continent except Australia and Antarctica. But it was in a region of North Africa where they were viewed as more than just animals. They were viewed as gods.

Felis silvestris catus is a descendent of African wildcats, which were attracted to ancient Egyptian cities where scrap food was abundant. Instead of banishing the felines, the Egyptians kept them around because they recognized the value of having a predator to kill the vermin that destroyed their crops. Appreciation thus became veneration.

The Egyptians called this creature *miu*, meaning "one that meows." After *miu* made its way into their homes and was handfed, it was tamed and became a domestic animal. When *mius* died, the owners displayed grief by shaving their eyebrows. Killing a *miu* was punishable by death, except, of course, when a priest offered up the *miu* as a sacrifice. Soon *mius* were represented in sculptures and painted on the walls of tombs. They were even mummified. The goddess Bastet was portrayed with the body of a woman and the head of a *miu*. She was believed to have two natures: one gentle and one vicious—perfect personifications of the pet. Thousands of mummified *mius* were buried at Bastet's temple. Centuries later when Bastet's temple was uncovered and the *miu*-mummies were unearthed, many were apathetically discarded, assumed worthless. Times were changing; the cat was becoming devalued.

At the other end of the desert in the seventh century, the cat slipped in status from that of a god to that of an animal, but it still enjoyed higher standing than other members of the animal kingdom. In Arabia, Islamic beliefs allowed cats to enter into mosques. Even today, while Muslim men and women have to perform ablutions before entering a mosque for prayer, cats, because they are innately hygienic, can waltz right in whenever they please. Muslims' Prophet Muhammad is said to have personally kept a cat named Muezza, who he sometimes stroked in his lap as he gave sermons to his followers. Muhammad was known to be respectful toward cats, treating them almost as though they were equal to humans, because one had saved him from a snake attack. Because of this, Muslims believe cats can enter paradise after they die.

But in medieval Europe, cats had a very grim fate. Associated with women, witchcraft and women in witchcraft, cats became scapegoats for devil-fearing worshippers. They were burned by the hundreds, thrown against walls and tortured in other horrifying ways. This hatred of cats lasted until the Enlightenment period, and after the first cat show in Britain in 1871, cats were accepted as pets. Our contemporary cat culture was born.

Today, cats are neither revered nor demonized. Instead of deifying or vilifying them, we humanize them. Two hundred million years after the genetic split, the two species have reunited.

We provide them with bowls, bathrooms, toys and beds, and dress them in clothes; some people who really want to transform their cats' image buy them Kitty Wigs. Around the world, we organize cat pageants and read cat magazines with sexy cat centerfolds, and some of us go so far as to perform cat yoga, a meditative exercise in which humans and cats can achieve transcendence together. When our feline friends become ill, we take them to vets, animal therapists or, if we still can't get to the core of our cat's problems, a pet psychic!

Cats are treated like members of the family. From the moment of ownership, you can insure your cat's health. You can take your cat to daycare and take it out to a cat café. If your cat goes missing, you can hire a pet detective. And in the terrible circumstance that your family falls apart, there are lawyers out there who will fight for you to have full or partial custody of your cat.

There are approximately five million domestic cats in Canada, and over 76 million in the United States, making them the largest visible minority in both countries. Well, okay, so maybe they don't count as a minority group until they're eligible to vote, but considering the degree to which our culture humanizes cats, they should be eligible to vote!

Actually, in Guffey, Colorado (population 26), cats can hold office. Monster is the sitting mayor of Guffey. Running as a "Democat," the cat was elected in 1998 after beating out canines from the "Repuplican" Party. Monster is the fourth mayoral feline in Guffey. There hasn't been another vote since he took office, which is actually a garage, so with him now in his 10th year of power, it's starting to look more like a dictatorship than a democracy. (Maybe that's why cats can't vote. They don't want to. They're communists.)

Even though they often impose on us, we still love our cats without stipulation. But what is it about cats that we admire? Does their aloofness and independence mirror our society's individualist ideals? Or perhaps we're jealous of their liberties and envy them their naps and their whimsy?

As you will learn in this book, cats instinctively possess many of our traits. Like us, they can feel ambitious, nurturing, alienated, powerful and weak. They can be heroes, adventurers, movie stars, criminals and even ghosts. It's more than the position of our eyes and the fact that we are both mammals that bring us together; it's our natural desire to want more out of life.

CHAPTER ONE

Domesticated Daredevils

NO DOUBT, THE LOVE THAT humans have for their cats is strong and unwavering, and though it may seem irrational, when you stand back and look at it objectively, the love is real. But how much—if at all—do our cats love us back?

Peruse the tucked-away sections of your newspaper and you'll find the occasional tale of a kitty going far and beyond to save the day. Short, human-interest segments at the tail end of your nightly news or simple "Did you hear…?" water-cooler conversations remind us of the unlimited dedication cats can have for their human companions. These stories of feline heroism prove that with a loving home and a strong relationship, our cats are willing to do for us anything within their power.

We've all heard this before: "our pets love us unconditionally." Personally, I don't buy it. I believe you have to earn their love.

I got my first cat, Feefee, when I was two. I was a terrible two, and I did terrible things to Feefee for two years. Some of my antics were to throw her down the stairs or practice wrestling moves on her. It's no wonder that Feefee never saved me from a dog attack, and she eventually ran away. She must have told the entire cat community about me, because throughout my life, almost every cat I've owned—Giuseppe, Cramer, India and Campbell—ran away from me as soon as they could, usually within a few months.

It wasn't until I was 20 years old that I found a cat that trusted me. He was a black and white tabby with varying gray streaks. He had the longest hair I've ever seen on a cat, and his perpetual fluff gave him the appearance of a collection of bellybutton lint accumulated over Christmas holidays.

His name was Kubrick. Either Kubrick didn't receive Feefee's memo, or he didn't care about my tarnished past; he loved me and was as affectionate with me as I was with him. So long as I always fed him and never surprised him with whatever dangerous maneuver I learned from Hulk Hogan, Kubrick was ready to defend me to the death. He displayed his vigilance time after time with my dates who came over and, after an encounter with my overprotective kitten, never visited again. But I forgave his overzealousness, and soon my gentle caring paid off.

One day, while I was writing at my office desk, Kubrick meowed for my attention. I looked down at him and said, "Not now, dude. I'm busy." I watched him walk back to the living room, and I continued to work. But only seconds later, he returned, rubbing his head against my ankle, meowing incessantly. I thought he wanted to play paw-boxing or watch a movie, or both, as he usually did.

"I can't play with you right now," I said. "I've got a deadline."

Again, Kubrick walked back to the living room and then returned. This time he started biting at my ankle.

"What?" I shouted. I stood up to intimidate him out of my office, and as I did, he scurried toward the living room again. I walked to the office door and reached to close it. Then I stopped. I smelled something burning.

I rushed out of my office, twisted around the corner and entered the living room. There was Kubrick, standing next to a small circle of smoke billowing from my carpet. It seems I had abandoned a cigarette, and it had fallen from the ashtray on the coffee table. I quickly snuffed out the fire and thanked my cat. Then we watched a movie and shared a bowl of buttery popcorn.

Cats do what they can to protect themselves and us. Sometimes their only means are to use their voice boxes and speak up. Kubrick knew this, and he saved himself and I, and hundreds of other apartment residents, from becoming homeless.

Calling For Help

In January 2006, Jean Poole of Manchester, Pennsylvania, was having an afternoon catnap with her nine-month-old granddaughter when her middle-aged feline, Princess, interrupted with constant, shrill meowing. Jean lay there, looking sideways at her cat, and as she slipped further out of her slumber, she realized that Princess' cantankerous pleas weren't all that she could hear. Somewhere in the adjacent room, Jean heard crackling. And as she gained more lucidity, she recognized the smell of smoke.

By the time the firefighters arrived, flames were shooting out of the roof. Luckily, Jean managed to grab the baby and escape out the rear door. And with barely any time to spare, she got Princess out of there, too.

The next cat was also brave, but not so lucky.

In 2002, a cat saved six families from an inferno in Essen, Germany. At 5:00 AM, just as the July sky was beginning to brighten, the feline woke her owner. Once the cat's cries finally penetrated the owner's slumber, she opened her eyes to the sight of flames and became aware of the smell of smoke. In a panic, the owner called the fire department, which rushed to the scene and knocked on the doors of all the building's occupants. The cat's actions saved everyone in the building, but sadly, she lost her life in the blaze. Her owner, who suffered from extreme smoke inhalation, managed to live and tell the story of her cat heroine.

Of course, one could argue that these so-called heroic felines are dependent on their owners for their survival—to dial for help, open a door or put out a burgeoning fire—and are therefore acting out of selfishness as much as selflessness. But consider another other German cat, one that used its voice to save a complete stranger who was weaker and more defenseless.

In April 2006, a Cologne resident was awakened in the middle of the night by a continuously meowing cat. Unable to get back to sleep, the homeowner rolled out of bed and opened the front door to shoo away the disruptive kitty. To the homeowner's surprise, an abandoned baby boy was waiting on the other side of the door, with a mysterious cat by his side. Police later stated that the cat saved the boy from life-threatening hypothermia.

Occasionally, cats see no difference between saving their human family, a human stranger or a stranger of another species entirely.

⚜

In England in October 2003, a lamb escaped from a pasture and clumsily collapsed into an outdoor swimming pool. It fell through the plastic sheet covering the pool and got its big head entangled in the cover's straps. Of course, the lamb couldn't swim, and neither could the only witness, a black and white, tail-less cat—or *moggy*, as Britons say—named Puss Puss.

Frenzied, Puss Puss charged back and forth between the pool and the garden, where her owners were working. The cat bombarded them with her agitated meows, to the point where her owners were agitated themselves. But knowing that Puss Puss had severe arthritis and wouldn't act in a physically exhausting manner unless absolutely necessary, they decided to follow her to the pool. When the owners found the drowning lamb, Puss Puss' human dad, Adrian Bunton, dove in and saved it. Had Puss Puss vocalized her pleas differently, the poor lamb may have remained in peril because not all meows are the same. With a hiss, a cat is saying, "I'm angry," but with meows, they could be saying one of three things: "I'm happy," "I'm hungry" or "I'm freaking out!" When trying to communicate the latter, some cats, like Puss Puss, meow as loudly and high pitched as possible, and they often repeatedly meow to call for help. The cat in this next story, however, gives "calling for help" another meaning entirely.

Cat-toid

Cats respond more promptly to long "e" sounds, such as in "Fuffy," "Mitsy," "Feefee" and, of course, "Kitty."

Man's Other Best Friend

Fifty-year-old Gary Rosheisen had a dilemma. There he lay, on the floor between his bed and his wheelchair, unable to reach the cord above his pillow that would promptly alert a paramedic. To make things worse, this was one of the few times he forgot to wear his medical-alert necklace. He really regretted that now.

Gary lived a lonesome life in his Columbus, Ohio, apartment. It was New Years Day, 2006, and he had no visitors. It was just he and his four-legged roommate, Tommy, who was around somewhere, probably licking his crotch and readying himself for a snug snooze against the radiator.

Gary's blood pressure was higher than it ought to be, so in 2002, he brought Tommy into his apartment to help bring it back down to an acceptable level. Gary also suffered from osteoporosis, and several minor strokes had left him wheelchair-bound, so he used whatever help was available, even if it was covered in hair and scratched up his furniture. To take Tommy's assistance one step further, Gary tried to teach him how to call for help. He programmed a speed-dial button with 911. Repeatedly, he pressed Tommy's paws over the speakerphone button and then the emergency speed-dial button. He always left the phone on the floor, level with Tommy, just in case a crisis occurred. Gary trained Tommy partly out of wishful thinking and partly for his own amusement.

He never actually expected Tommy to understand or even care to understand.

However, at that moment, with Gary wedged between the chair and bed, it was showtime for Tommy.

But Gary wondered if the cat even knew his owner was in distress. If Tommy saw him now, he'd probably just think Gary was enjoying the floor in much the same way Tommy did on these cozy winter evenings. *Oh, how very much we have in common, roomie!*

So Gary lay there on the floor. Weighing his options, he decided he could either wait patiently for another visitor, maybe come Easter, or he could start screaming for help. He did neither because, after only 10 minutes, there was a knock at the door.

The person knocking identified himself as Officer Patrick Daugherty. He asked, "Is there a problem here?"

"Yeah, I'm on the floor!" Gary shouted from his bedroom. And then he paused, dumbfounded. Thinking out loud, he said, "But how did you know about that?"

Officer Daugherty didn't know about Gary's situation. All he knew was that a 911 dispatcher received a phone call from this specific number and this specific address. When pressed for a reply, the caller had said nothing. All the dispatcher could hear was the room ambiance at the other end of the line, so being cautious, the dispatcher sent for help.

When Daugherty entered the apartment, he saw an orange-and-white striped shorthair cat gazing at him patiently, sitting on the living room floor next to a phone. The police officer stepped past the cat and followed the man's voice into the room where he lay stranded. After helping Gary into his chair, the men immediately discussed the mystery caller's identity.

Baffled, they concluded that the only possibility was Tommy, whom Gary now calls his hero.

Winnie the Wondercat

In New Castle, Indiana, in April 2006, Kathy Keesling awoke in an unusual state. It was almost 4:00 AM, and her cat, Winnie, a 14-year-old American shorthair—usually haughty and aloof—was aggressively, almost violently, clawing away at her. The cat was batting and scratching, jumping all over her owner and the bed, pulling Kathy's hair with her puffy paws. Kathy had no idea how long Winnie had been trying to disturb her slumber, but the scratches and bites suggested several minutes. This peculiarity, along with feeling like she'd been whacked across the head with an aluminum bat, was enough for Kathy's intuition to tell her something was wrong.

In her drowsy and blurry-eyed state, Kathy saw that her husband, Eric, was still asleep on the other side of the bed. She wheezed out of the covers,

Peer into the alert eyes of Winnie.

~⚭~

stumbled to a telephone and dialed 911. She
explained that she had just been woken up by her
cat and that she felt dizzy and sluggish—to which
the 911 dispatcher prompted Kathy to get herself
and her family out of the house immediately. Kathy
vigorously shook her husband into consciousness.
Her son, Michael, only four months older than
Winnie, was still in his downstairs bed, breathing,
but completely knocked out. He had to be carried
out of the house.

After the ambulance arrived, a total analysis
of the scene was conducted. The results surprised
the Keeslings, but not the medics.

Earlier that week, the Keeslings' basement had flooded with 30,000 gallons of water. Eric, a volunteer firefighter, had used a gas pump to remove the water. At some point in the cleaning process, something went wrong. Small but deadly amounts of carbon monoxide gas had slowly leaked into the home, filled the basement and moved up the stairs into the master bedroom. Michael, whose bedroom was closest to the leak, had inhaled a much higher amount of the gas than his parents.

Carbon monoxide levels of two to three percent are fatal for humans. Michael's body tested at six percent. The medics informed the Keeslings that if they had endured just five more minutes of the poison, the entire family would have died. The family owed their lives to Winnie. If it weren't for her enhanced feline senses—a multitude of nose receptors that can detect odors too subtle for any human—and a steadfast insistence that Kathy get up and get out of there, the story would be a tragedy, and Winnie would probably be an orphan again, if not dead herself.

What inspired Winnie to act so courageously? Obviously, Winnie needed someone to open the house door and get her out of there too. So is that why she was so persistent in trying to wake Kathy? Perhaps it was an act of love, a result of the connection that had developed between Winnie and her family over their 10-year companionship. Maybe, just maybe, it was an act of gratitude, a special thank you to the family that once saved her own little life.

One July day in 1993, Kathy was on a neighbor's farm when she heard a chirping peep from the grass by the barn. Expecting to find some chicks, Kathy homed in on the sound, and to her surprise found a lone kitten. Just three days old, the kitty's eyes were still shut and her body still hairless. Who and where the kitten's mother was seemed like a useless question to ask. Indiana's rural areas are filled with feral cats, and it's likely this one was forgotten. Forgotten by all but Kathy, who scooped up the orphan and brought her home.

When her husband arrived home later that day, Kathy said to him, "We have a visitor." At the time, the Keeslings were regular participants in a child foster program, so Eric assumed the visitor was another foster child. When he was introduced to the kitten, he was charmed and warmed by her vulnerability. He had no problem with taking the kitten in, and besides, he already had a four-month-old baby boy, so how much trouble could it be?

Kathy realized that raising the kitten would be more difficult than expected. Because the kitten was so dependent, Kathy had to nurse it to health. As she did with her baby, Michael, she filled a bottle with milk and fed the kitten. She spent several nights with the tiny creature, ensuring she was well cared for. Kathy admits, "I didn't think she was gonna make it."

But she did. She has lived long enough to be named Winnie, after the female lead in the TV series *The Wonder Years*. Years went by, and Winnie continued to charm the Keesling family and whatever visitors they had. She has lived long enough to repay the Keeslings for rescuing her, and as if being a lifesaver is not enough, Winnie also displays some uncanny speaking skills, according to Kathy. "People think I'm nuts, but she actually talks sometimes." And Kathy doesn't mean "talk" as in a sophisticated meowing of sorts, nor does she mean "talk" as in metaphorical communication based on trust and gesticulations. When Kathy says Winnie can talk, she means the cat can actually speak…English!

Kathy says that when Winnie is thirsty, she jumps on the counter, stands by the sink and says "waaa'er." When Winnie can't be seen, Kathy need only holler, "Winnie, where are you?" and she swears that she can hear the cat respond, "Right hee—eere!" Allegedly, when the local Channel Six News filmed a segment on Winnie for her amazing bravery, Winnie could be heard on video, however abstractly, defending her privacy by pleading to the crew, "Leave me al-ooooone."

Winnie's courage and protection of her family garnered her an award from the American Society for the Prevention of Cruelty to Animals (ASPCA).

Winnie poses with her family, Kathy, Eric and Michael Keesling, at the ASPCA ceremony in New York, 2007.

~⊙⊂~

In recognition of her unique bravery, the Keesling family—Kathy, Eric, Michael and Winnie—were flown to New York City to collect the prize. On top of that, they were treated lavishly for three days, all expenses paid. They were put in the luxurious Manhattan Marriott Hotel right in Times Square, and the awards ceremony itself cost $1000 per plate. Quite a change from the lifestyle they live in New Castle (population 40,000), where Eric works as a truck driver and Kathy works as a truck stop cashier.

At the ASPCA ceremony, Winnie left a huge impression on the attendees, adorned in her black and purple cape with the white letter "W" sewn on it. The Keeslings and their friends call her "Winnie the Wondercat." Along with a dog named Toby, who saved his choking owner by jumping on her chest until a piece of apple dislodged from her throat, Winnie received a large trophy for her efforts. Her trophy had the words "Cat of the Year 2007" engraved on it.

Kitty Cops

Cats are often stereotyped as being lazy because they spend half of each average day asleep. But cats are hunters, and when your kitty dozes off, he or she is conserving energy—which could end up saving your life. Leonard Rzepnicki knows this firsthand.

In December 2003, Leonard and his wife Cheryl Walker were entertaining three friends in the kitchen of their New York apartment, dining on a smorgasbord of beans and neck bones. As well as the five of them, there was a sixth individual named Booboo Kitty lurking around somewhere on all fours. There was a knock at the door. *It must be more guests,* thought the hosts.

Leonard looked through the peephole. It was a friend of a friend, which made the man welcome in Leonard's home. He opened the door to invite him in, but another man suddenly came into view, a man who Leonard did not know. Leonard looked at his new friend's face and saw wide-eyed worry. He then looked at the stranger; the man was holding a gun against the friend's back.

The armed man pushed himself inside, slamming the door behind him. With his gun pointed at the group, he demanded they all strip naked. They did as they were told. The armed man then demanded all they hand over all their valuables and cash. That, Leonard told him, was something they couldn't do. They were all very poor and had nothing to hand over. After all, they lived in the rough part of Manhattan.

Yet, despite the neighborhood and the meager meal laid out on the table, the would-be robber didn't believe them. He ordered Leonard to take him to the bedroom so that he could go through the dresser drawers, but Leonard was petrified. The robber pointed the gun at Leonard's face, but Leonard still couldn't move. The armed man began searching for anything of value, but then he looked at his feet and spotted Booboo Kitty standing curiously before the nudists in the kitchen.

The partygoers begged the robber not to hurt Booboo, but the man saw the cat as the perfect defenseless hostage. He picked her up with his free hand. She warned him with a hiss. He continued trying to brandish her as an example to the others, but Booboo Kitty lived by a two-strike rule. She swiftly scratched his hand, and he dropped her.

The cat scampered into the bedroom, and the robber, too proud to let her get away, chased after her. That's when Leonard made his stark-naked dash out of the apartment to a neighbor's place and called for help.

The police arrived and stormed Leonard's 10th floor apartment. He heard them marching up the stairs and down the hallway. Suddenly, a barrage of bullets echoed through the floors. The gunman was dead. The partygoers were still alive, all because of one daring cat, Booboo Kitty, who survived without receiving a booboo.

❧◆☙

In March 2002, a courageous cat from Lansing, Michigan, saved its owner, a seven-year-old-girl, from a sexual predator. The little girl was playing in her yard with her cat, which she viewed as her very best friend, but she really had no idea just how valuable a friend it was. Not until she came face to face with a predator.

Her neighbor, Mr. Lopez, approached the girl and lured her into his home with fake promises. She wasn't about to leave her kitty behind, so the girl innocently followed Lopez, holding her cat snug in her arms. She wasn't the least bit afraid; he was her neighbor, after all, and she was taught that adults know best. But soon after entering Lopez's home, she learned that he was a very bad man.

He attacked the girl, and she dropped the cat. The cat scrambled as Lopez held the child down and put duct tape over her mouth to silence her. From across the room, the cat watched helplessly as the man tried to hurt its friend. When Lopez tried to remove the girl's clothes, the cat could bear it no more. It attacked.

The girl was trying desperately to free herself from Lopez's grip when she heard her attacker yowl in pain. Her cat was scratching at his arms, and while he tried to swat it away, the girl escaped. She ran out the door with the cat following closely behind. She immediately told an adult—one that she could trust.

When the police arrived, they found Lopez hiding in his crawl space. Not only did the cat save its owner from a harrowing experience, but it probably saved the other children in the neighborhood as well.

❧◆☙

Veterinarian Steven Vassall was a fraud and a petty larcenist. An unemployed lab technician, he had practiced on animals without a license for years, often injuring them. Pet owners appreciated the convenience of a vet who made house calls to pick up and deliver their pets. They had no idea that his clinic was actually just his apartment.

Steven knew that he could get away with it because, obviously, the animals could not speak—animals such as Fred, the shorthair kitten whom Steven was paid $135 cash to neuter. What Steven didn't know, though, was that Fred was an "undercover cop" and that his "owner" was actually his partner.

In 2005, Fred was rescued as a kitten by New York's Animal Care & Control. When he was found, he had a collapsed lung and pneumonia. Assistant District Attorney Carol Moran adopted him and helped him regain his health. After his recovery, Fred began working with the Brooklyn District Attorney's office and the New York Police Department.

His mission came the following February. He was to bring down the suspected criminal, Steven Vassall. Fred was hired as a decoy animal patient, and after the sting went down successfully, the fake vet was charged with unauthorized veterinary practice, criminal mischief, injuring animals and petty larceny.

District Attorney Charles J. Hynes awarded Fred the Law Enforcement Appreciation Award, and the cat was also honored with the Mayor's Alliance Award. Aside from these awards, the actress Mary Tyler Moore gave a tribute to Fred during a pet adoption benefit.

After the bust, Fred retired from law enforcement and was to begin a career in pet therapy. Sadly, before he could begin his new position, he was struck and killed by a motorist. He will always be remembered for his bravery as the "Undercover Kitty."

Amy Spencer had just moved into her new apartment in Austin, Texas, in January 2008. She was settling in with her friend and her cat Sophie. Sophie was checking out the new home thoroughly, learning all the cool new hiding places, the rumpus areas and the best spaces for leverage when jumping.

Sophie hopped onto the kitchen counter and then onto the pantry cupboard above the fridge, pacing back and forth in the gap between the pantry and ceiling—probably pondering how to get back down. Amy observed her stranded, rambunctious cat but noticed that she was pawing and pushing her nose against something up there. It sounded like plastic sliding against the wood. Amy drafted her taller friend to grab the cat and investigate. She advised her friend to be careful; after all, it could be rat poison or a rat trap up there.

Her friend retrieved seven DVDs, all unlabelled and without cases. They put one in the recently hooked-up DVD player and watched. At first, they thought it was an ordinary home movie, but within seconds they realized just how virulent and despicable the movies were. It was child pornography.

Horrified, Amy and her friend reported the findings to the landlord. Using an email address the landlord had been given by the former tenants, and with the landlord's help, police contacted one of the two roommates who had lived in the apartment. The female roommate gave the police permission to search her computer, which she shared with her male roommate, who denied owning the DVDs. Sure enough, police found the evidence they needed to arrest the male roommate and garner a confession from him.

Although Sophie couldn't do anything to protect the abused children in the videos, by leading authorities to the owner of the DVDs, she helped lock away a man who might have one day taken his deplorable obsession one step further.

Crime Writer/Crime Fighter

They say that when someone loses one of their five senses, the other four strengthen. Agatha Christie—not the famed novelist, but the black, white and ginger-swirl calico—is a testament to this theory. Agatha, or Aggie as her companion Lynn Seely, a writer and professional runner, calls her, was born with an eye infection that left her blind. Despite her disability, Aggie displayed a scrappiness that was second to none. Maybe the tiny kitten had the feline version of "little man syndrome," being aggressive to compensate for her size, or maybe in her risky world with the odds stacked against her, she was ready to fight for her survival. Or perhaps it was her roughhousing brothers who had brought out the spunk in her.

Aggie lived on a Pennsylvania farm, the only female of five fluffy kittens. As a result of her eye infection, her life was endangered—not because she was blind, but because the farmer whose

barn she lived in considered her an invalid. Under-
estimating her, he automatically assumed she was
useless and decided that she was better off dead.
He informed his wife that he would be "putting her
out of her misery" by putting her in a bag and
drowning her. But behind her husband's back, the
wife snuck out to the barn and saved Aggie. She
took the kitten to an elderly neighbor who ran an
animal sanctuary, who in turn called Lynn.

The new softhearted owner was completely
enamored by Aggie's charisma and stamina.
Lynn was impressed by Aggie's ability to cope
with her blindness and do most of the things
other cats do, most importantly finding the litter
box. But there were difficulties, of course, the
biggest of which was Aggie's inability to descend
stairs. The struggle didn't come about as a result of
her blindness, but her size. She was too small
to reach down and transfer her weight from stair to
stair. So Aggie would calmly wait for Lynn to come
to get her every time she was stranded.

Lynn didn't mind the kitten's arrested development. She was patient with Aggie and saw
a challenge where most would see a nuisance.
Instead of leaving Aggie as she was, Lynn rehabilitated her and taught her, literally step by step,
how to descend the stairs. With those lessons,
Aggie learned to trust Lynn.

Aggie grew up to be a large, able cat. By the
time she was three years old, she had mastered

everything a cat her age needed to master. And her blindness may have enhanced her extrasensory abilities to spot danger, too.

One night, footsteps in the alley approached the kitchen window and stopped. In a tunnel of the seven-foot-tall cat tree that Lynn kept in the kitchen, Aggie slept. Behind the cat tree was a window facing the back alley. As soon as Aggie's ears sensed something peculiar on the other side of that window, her eyes widened, and she stared unseeingly into the pitch black, as she always had since birth. The window screen started to rattle, and then the click of its removal penetrated Aggie's senses.

The cool air seeped in. Aggie continued to listen, bracing herself for what came next. She understood it couldn't be Lynn or her husband John; they were sleeping upstairs, so far unperturbed by the faint disturbance.

There was a heavy *plop*, and then another as cinder blocks were stacked below the window. The fur on Aggie's body stood on end.

Something scraped the top of the blocks—feet standing to gain leverage. Aggie crawled closer to the edge of her cat tunnel but remained hidden. Two solid *slaps* hit the edge of the windowsill—human hands about to lift the rest of the human body inside.

Aggie's claws protruded.

The intruder hauled himself onto the window-sill, and with his feet secured on the edge, all he had to do to begin his robbery was take a simple step forward into the house. Aggie pounced. She attached herself to his head, sunk her claws into his face and then leapt safely back to the floor. The robber was so startled, so pained, that he fell back-wards into the alley, leaving a shoe neatly on the windowsill.

His sudden scream alerted the sleeping family, and they rushed downstairs. They saw an open window, a stranded shoe and blood on Aggie's paws and cat tree. What had taken place didn't sink in right away, but as Lynn's heart rate slowed to a normal rhythm, she was able to piece together what had happened.

It was obvious; Aggie had selflessly put her life on the line for the safety of her loving owners.

Lynn called the police, but the robber was never positively identified. However, police were pretty sure that they had caught the guy, when a month after the incident, a man named Jack was arrested for selling stolen property. The police connected the deep scratches on his face to the break and enter at the Seely home, but even with the shoe found on the windowsill, there was not enough evidence to charge him with the specific crime. If Aggie could see, maybe she could have pointed him out in a lineup.

The robber became the butt of many jokes, both by police and other criminals. They dubbed him "Attack Cat Jack."

Little Agatha Christie also got another little nickname: "Pet Hero of the Year 2002." The story of her blind bravery appeared on the front pages of two newspapers, and she was featured on two TV shows, *Miracle Pets* and *Animal Miracles*. Of course, she gave Lynn plenty to write about, too. Lynn wrote about Aggie in a short story titled "Blind but Brave" in the book *Faithful Guardians*. Sometimes the smallest things are our biggest inspirations.

Cat-toid

A Himalayan-Persian named Tinker Toy, fully grown at 7.5 inches long and 2.75 inches tall, is the smallest cat to have ever lived, according to the *Guinness World Records* book.

CHAPTER TWO

Miracle Mousers

ALTHOUGH SOME EXTRAORDINARY cats will watch your back and do their best to protect you, they still need help from their human companions. Cats are naturally curious and often find themselves in sticky situations. Up in trees, trapped in walls, their heads stuck in peanut butter jars—the dilemmas they get themselves into tread a fine line between adventurousness and stupidity.

Such was the case with Jinksy of Cambridgeshire, England, in 2006. His owners David and Shirley Matthews had no idea how their six-month-old kitten found his way onto their apartment roof, but he did. And while investigating the roof for treats and toys, he fell through a two-inch gap and became wedged between the building and the neighbor's home. His distressed pleas for help found their way to the ears of the Matthews. Standing over the gap, they realized that he was too deep to be reached by hand and too elevated to free-fall safely. Luckily for Jinksy, his human parents loved him very much and destroyed part of the wall to save him.

A cat from Indiana named Droopy got himself in an icy situation because he didn't follow the typical cat stereotypes. Although most cats don't like water and will claw anything that brings it near their faces, Droopy relished it. He loved water so much that he wanted to play in it, even in winter. Unfortunately, Droopy never learned the first thing about thermodynamics, so when he saw something that looked like water, he assumed it was liquid and not ice. One cold February day in 2007, Droopy was exploring the yard, as he did often, unnoticed by his owners, who trusted his wits. But when his owner, Melissa Jones, went outside for a cigarette, she discovered him stuck in an ice puddle from the hind legs down. She ran inside the house and fetched her husband, as well as buckets of hot water to melt the ice. They managed to free Droopy, but it's unlikely he'll be swimming again.

◦◦◆◦◦

And then there's Emerald, a Staten Island cat who, in 2006, spent more than one day perched on a three-story utility pole, wired with 25,000 volts of electricity. Unlike Jinsky and Droopy, Emerald's dilemma was not the fault of her curiosity, but rather her own instinctual defense mechanism. When she was outside playing in the yard, two stray dogs came along, looked at her and saw an uncanny resemblance to lunch. They chased her, and naturally, her primal instincts told her to climb. *Climb what though? How about this tall metal tree.* The dogs fled, but now Emerald had to find her way down.

Her owner tried calling the electric company, but they weren't available until the next day. So Emerald spent 38 hours clinging on for dear life until the workers showed up and brought her down safely to her owner's arms.

Amazingly, Emerald could have probably spent 38 *days* on that pole, as long as she did not mess with the power-charged wires. The fat stored in a cat's body allows it to endure long periods—sometimes up to seven or eight weeks—without a bite to eat. They can absorb water from condensation, and their stomachs feed on their excess fat. Of course, I'm not advocating you start starving your cat to save money—when cats are hungry, their search for food will probably put them in a sticky situation that you could do without.

Cat-toid

A Millbury cat with two names, Frank and Louie, grew up to be a fully grown, healthy adult, despite having two faces. Two-headed cats are rare, and they almost never live more than a few weeks. Frank and Louie—the two-nosed, two-mouthed, three-eyed miracle—is currently eight years old.

I'll Have What the Humans Are Having

Tabitha Cain and her parents are not cat owners, but they do love the little critters. So much so that they generously put out food at their Bartlett, Tennessee, home for six feral cats that roam freely in their neighborhood. The cats have grown to appreciate the Cain family, except for Wild Oats—a short-tempered, scaredy-cat.

But one warm winter day in 2007, when Tabitha went out to feed the kitties, she spotted Wild Oats in a sticky situation. Somehow, Oats got his chubby head stuck in a peanut butter jar, probably while scavenging for food, since he won't eat from the Cain's pantry. When Tabitha went to help the clumsy critter, he would not, as always, let her anywhere near him. He ran away, dragging himself and the massive contraption on his cranium to a hiding spot where she couldn't get her hands on him.

Tabitha notified her parents, and together the family tried to emancipate Oats from the devilish jar. But their efforts were to no avail.

Throughout the week, every time they saw him, they'd try to catch the cat so they could get the jar off his head. After almost two weeks, Wild Oats disappeared. He was presumed dead, starved or suffocated.

But on the 19th day of his ordeal, they found him. He was skinnier than ever. He was weak and, most importantly for them, he was slow. Using a fishing net, the Cains were able to catch and restrain him. He didn't put up much of a fight, because, as it seems, he was ready for help.

They oiled his dirty neck and managed to slip his head through the jar opening. Wild Oats was saved, but the Cains weren't about to let him get into any more mishaps. Not yet, anyway. They brought him home and put him in a cage. They treated the wounds he received as they squeezed and pulled his head out of the jar, and gave him water for a week, until he was strong enough to eat.

Once Wild Oats was healthy again, they let him back into the wild, where nothing could tame him.

A Precious Discovery

It's hard to imagine what was going through D.J. Kerr's mind. The Manhattan woman was out of town with her husband, Steve, on the morning of September 11, 2001, when she and the entire world first witnessed the televised horror. Her apartment was in a seven-story high-rise directly across from the World Trade Center. When the towers tumbled and the impact sent a destructive wave throughout the vicinity, she could probably envision her windows shattering from the shock wave.

There were too many thoughts scrambled in her head to put in order. Her city was under attack. Thousands of people were dead. Her home was destroyed. Was another attack going to occur?

Would it be near her home? Her cat was...where *was* her cat?

Her Persian, Precious, was home alone waiting for a house sitter to attend to her at 10:00 AM. For a moment, D.J. probably feared for the life of the house sitter before she remembered that it was too early in the morning, and the sitter would be safe in her own home. But still, the cat was alone in a destroyed building—trapped somewhere in a room that was probably now filled with glass, metal, toxic dust and smoke.

Believing that it would be impossible for Precious to survive, D.J. accepted that her cat was a casualty of the worst attack on American soil.

After the attacks, volunteers took over "The Pile" and began the rescue effort. But as the days and weeks went by, the rescue effort became a cleanup. Whatever was left in the debris could only be buried. However, after 18 days of diligence, a rescue team of humans and dogs made a startling discovery. Volunteers heard the desperate cries of a cat from atop a building, and a rescue team was sent to the cluttered rooftop to investigate. What their feet and paws stepped through seemed to them to be just more piles of dusty drywall and glass, an amalgamation of the Twin Towers and several other structures in the neighborhood. They didn't know D.J., nor were they aware that below their feet was her home. And in with the wreckage was her most prized possession.

Nobody is quite sure how Precious ended up on the roof, but there she was. Once a white Persian with long curly hair, she now had smoke-stained fur. The frightened cat proved hard to catch even though it was weak and had gone without food for three weeks. A recovery dog helped corner Precious, making escape impossible. Although it was probably the most terrifying moment Precious had experienced since the attacks, it all paid off.

Precious was placed a nearby van owned by Suffolk County SPCA, which was on-site to treat the rescue dogs. Amazingly, the workers found that she was going to be fine, even though her lungs were filled with dust and smoke, she had a damaged eye and a burned paw from the smoldering debris, her mouth was covered with sores and she was severely dehydrated. (The sores were the result of what had actually saved her: lapping up dirty water.) And after being reunited with the Kerrs, Precious was back to her favorite daily diet of sliced turkey.

Cat-toid

Despite their relatively small sizes, cats' bodies have 290 bones—the human body has only 206. Ten percent of cats' bones are in their tails, which is vital for good balance.

Just Like One of Us

In southern Oregon, Little Draggin' Bear was found lying on the ground in pain, after a bullying raccoon attacked him. A local Ashland student found the ash-gray, longhair kitten sprawled out and crying for help. The poor cat couldn't move. When the student picked him up, Draggin' Bear's hind legs dangled limply in the air. He was rushed to the nearest animal clinic and brought to the attention of Dr. Alice Davis.

Alice knew almost immediately that the cat had suffered a broken back. An x-ray confirmed that Little Draggin' Bear would never walk again. All he could do was drag himself across the floor, a sad sight for the veterinarian and anyone else who witnessed it. Although most animal hospitals would euthanize an animal in his condition, Alice looked into Draggin' Bear's big, dark, almond-shaped eyes and saw hope.

She adopted him and took him home to her fiancé, Gordon Sievers. They named him Little Draggin' Bear because of his mode of transportation, and because Alice worked at Bear Creek Animal Clinic. But she couldn't stand to see him sliding around his whole life. So she and Gordon brainstormed ways of making him a big walkin' bear.

Gordon went online and researched possible treatments. He figured if human paraplegics could be given mobility with the use of wheelchairs, the same could be done for a cat. He ordered a construction set for elementary engineers and built a plastic cart out of the multicolored plastic pieces, attaching four red and yellow wheels to its sides. Using a head-band, he made a sling that supported Draggin' Bear's body and then belted him in with Velcro straps.

It worked beautifully. With his legs hanging over the end of the "Draggin' Wagon," Draggin' Bear started wheeling himself around the house and clinic, completely unaware that he was different than the other cats he met. Alice says he's the most playful kitten she's ever seen. He loves to play with his tetherball and lounge in a sink or basket when he's not in his cart.

Of course, despite his mobility and unwavering exuberance, Draggin' Bear still requires special treatment. Alice kindly helps him to go to the litter box and has fitted him with a device that contains his uncontrollable bowel movements.

As Draggin' Bear grows, Gordon makes him larger carts to suit him more comfortably. Thanks to Gordon's invention and Alice's charity, Little Draggin' Bear is now four years old. At Bear Creek, he has become a mascot. Although his peers don't particularly like him and his wheeling ways, the children absolutely adore him.

Meow Tse-Tung

It was a regular May morning at Olympia Moto Sports, located in Hendersonville, North Carolina. General manager Eric Congdon opened the store bright and early and signed off on a new ship-ment of padded motorcycle clothes. He cut open

China lurks in the barn rafters, where she spends most, if not all, of her time.

~∞❌∞~

the cardboard box and pushed aside the flaps. Something inside the cargo moved frantically, startling him.

Eric jumped back, regained his composure and approached the box again, this time warily. He peeked inside. Two glowing eyes stared right back at him.

Inside the shipment was a weak, bony, terrified Oriental cat. The strange-looking creature, orange and gray striped with black feet, was skittish and unapproachable. Eric was surprised that it had been able to breathe in the box and had survived as long as it did without food or water. If this were a shipment of beef jerky and bottled water, it would make more sense. But Eric was in the automotive industry, and as far as he knew, no animal can live off of Kevlar.

What amazed Eric most was the journey the cat must have taken to find itself in the store. The shipment of motorcycle gear was an international import.

As it turns out, the cat was a Chinese immigrant. Thirty-five days earlier, on April 3, 2007, in Shanghai, it had chewed its way through the cardboard box, which was then loaded with others into a 40-foot-long cargo container that was in turn bolted shut. The cargo left China and sailed across the Pacific Ocean to the west coast of the United States. It was then literally driven across the country to the east coast and dropped off at Eric's shop.

Very few animals could survive such harsh conditions, but sometimes it pays to be a feline.

Eric named his miracle discovery "China," after the nation of its birth.

Before an American could adopt little China, she had to endure another 180 days with Henderson County Animal Services, because state law says foreign animals must be quarantined and vaccinated for six months prior to being sold or adopted out. After those six months were up, Deborah Couch, stepsister to Kevin Rhea—CEO of Olympia Moto Sports—and her husband, Allen, took China into their home.

After her month-long cargo incarceration, and half-year quarantine, China was a very shaky kitty. Placing China in a carrier, Deborah and Allen drove

China to her new home. China must have been absolutely stunned when she arrived at a four-acre farm in Glendale, Kentucky. Coming from a city with a population of over 20 million to a community of just 300, China adapted to her new life as a barn cat. It may not have been the big city life, but at least she had plenty of mice to chase. And it worked out for both China and the Couchs; they had a mouse problem, and China loved mice.

China is still skittish and unsociable, but she's grown into a muscular and athletic cat. She spends most of her time in the barn rafters, and the first time she ventured out, she was chased up a tree by the family's Jack Russell terrier.

Even now, Deborah says that China will only come within 10 feet of her owners. "She moves across the ground like a puma or cougar," says Deborah. "I think I will eventually get her somewhat tamed."

And with every day that goes by, China comes closer. Inch by inch, she is learning to trust the Couchs. Deborah says she just enjoys seeing China, however rarely, and knowing that she is alive and well, still in the barn and exterminating the mice. Since she moved onto their property, the family hasn't uncovered any mice droppings, and that's about all you can ask for from a mouser.

Tiger Hunting

In the mid-1980s, Mr. and Mrs. Whitaker were members of the U.S. Armed Forces, stationed at

a base in Ramstein, Germany. After three years
in Germany, their term had ended, and they
were being re-stationed in the U.S. Problem was,
it was possible they'd have to leave without their
six-month-old yellow tabby, Tiger.

Tiger was not neutered and had a reputation for
fickle wandering in pursuit of a girlfriend. So Nancy
Whitaker had him sequestered in a bathroom while
the movers packed their belongings, which would
be shipped to the States. They left specific notes in
German for the movers not to use that bathroom.
The movers didn't listen. Somebody opened the
bathroom door, and Tiger made a run for it.

The Whitakers had only four days to find Tiger.
They searched every crescent and pocket of the
neighborhood. They put up signs. They had friends
on the lookout. No luck.

But on the second day, just as they were giving
up hope, a neighbor called and said, "I think your
cat is in the boiler room of our building."

Colonel Whitaker wasted no time. He drafted
a friend to help him and followed up on the tip.
When they got to the boiler room, the men got on
all fours and crawled to where the cat was. It was
dark and dirty, but they could definitely make out
the shape of a feline. They reached toward the boiler
to grab the cat. Whitaker was scratched and his
friend was bitten, but when they grabbed a hold of
the cat's leg and pulled it into the light, they learned
that they had endured the attack in vain. It was

not Tiger. And despite his heavy-duty gloves, Whitaker was left with a scar from the stray.

The next day, as Nancy was leaving her home on the way to a going-away party, she received a call from someone at the base. "We understand that your husband was scratched by a stray cat."

"That's right," said Nancy.

"Well, he's going to have to go to the hospital and get rabies shots."

Nancy thought it was a joke that someone from her office was pulling on them. But it wasn't. The friend who was bitten by the cat had already gotten his shots and had informed officials that Colonel Whitaker was also at risk.

Nancy continued to argue the point. "Thank you," she said, "but no, I don't think it's necessary to do that."

"No, ma'am," said the caller, "you don't understand. Your husband is basically government property. If he's been subjected to rabies, he has to show up or we'll send a squad car out for him."

That was all she needed to hear. Colonel Whitaker got his first of many painful rabies shots, even though they were poised to leave the next day.

The Whitakers had to end their search for Tiger. Together with their six- and seven-year-old sons, they grabbed their suitcases and headed to the airport, leaving behind a cat carrier with some friends who, just in case Tiger was found, could ship him to America on the Whitakers' coin.

When they arrived home in the U.S., the Whitakers traveled across the country in an RV, visiting with family and friends, catching up on the country they'd missed dearly and occasionally stopping at various hospitals so Colonel Whitaker could complete his rabies shots.

They knew that Tiger was irreplaceable, but their sons missed their cat, so to appease the boys, they adopted a female kitten named Stubbie from a Virginia farm owned by Nancy's in-laws. After four weeks on the road, the Whitakers and Stubbie drove to their new home at Montgomery Air Force Base in Alabama. It was a sweltering 100° F in the first week of July, a huge contrast from the German breeze they'd been accustomed to for the last three years.

As they were wiping the sweat beads off their foreheads, they got a phone call from a woman in Germany. "We think we've found Tiger," she told Nancy. "He's in the pound and has been there for thirty days. It looks just like him, fits the description. Do you want us to ship him home?"

The Whitakers were absolutely delighted, but when they thought about the trouble and cost of shipping him back, and the fact that they had a new kitten and the children no longer missed Tiger, they couldn't just give the go-ahead on the spot. Besides, they had so much on their minds, now that they were back in America with a home to furnish.

"They're going to put him down if nobody claims him," said the woman on the phone. Before Nancy could respond, the caller continued, "Look, if you don't want him, I'll keep him."

"We need to think about it," said Nancy, satisfied that, at the very least, Tiger would be saved from euthanization and would have a good home. The next day, she and her family realized how fortunate it was that they'd held off.

The Whitakers' furniture arrived from its trip across the Atlantic. In big wooden crates, everything they had owned in Germany waited to be unpacked. Nancy recalls the scene like it was yesterday:

"These big, burly moving men took a crow bar and got the door off the crate. We immediately started to hear this horrible sound. I remembered that our kids had had this game that they left the batteries in on one of our previous moves. It made this repeating laughter or whoopee cushion sound." So Nancy and her family began digging through the boxes looking for the obnoxious toy. Once they found it, they turned it off and continued with the arduous process of unpacking their furnishings.

Shortly afterwards, one of the movers approached Nancy and asked, "Do you have a cat?"

"Yeah," she responded, "in the campground in the RV." She wondered how he knew that.

Surely Stubbie hadn't made an escape like Tiger had. The last six weeks had already been already complicated enough. The last thing they needed was to hunt for another pet.

The mover, noticing the confusion on Nancy's face, told her that there was something in the truck—not in the campground—and he was not getting back in there until it was gone. Nancy figured it was a raccoon or a rat that had crawled into the crate in Germany, but she was surprised that the mover was so apprehensive about it.

"As soon as we looked in that crate," recalls Nancy, "it all came together. The German movers had put our mattresses and box springs inside individual cartons. One of the ends of the box spring cartons was just eaten off and clawed to pieces." Through the shredded hole in the carton, they heard what sounded like that horrible, laughing toy again. But that was impossible. They toy was shut off and inside the house.

The movers pulled out the box spring carton, and Colonel Whitaker cut a hole in it with his pocket knife. When the hole was big enough, he reached in and, when he pulled out his hand, he was holding Tiger.

Tiger, who weighed 14 pounds only 40 days earlier, had shriveled to a bony 4 pounds. His fur was dirty, knotted and nasty. His skin hung off his skeleton like a kangaroo pouch. His eyes were dry and fixed open, unblinking. He smelled rancid after having turned the mattress into his bathroom and bed for over a month and spending the last couple days in 100° F weather,

"He meowed and meowed with every bit of life left in him," recalled Nancy.

Colonel Whitaker rushed to get the emaciated cat a bowl of water. Tiger quickly lapped it up. For food, all they had was some leftover pizza from lunch. They broke it up in pieces and fed it to Tiger. He devoured the pizza, too, only it came back up on the pavement. He was too weak to eat.

The Whitakers and the movers scooped up Tiger and rushed him to the vet. When they explained to the animal doctor what had happened, he didn't believe it. By coincidence, another family, whom the Whitakers knew from Germany, was at the animal hospital with their cat, so they could corroborate the wild story.

Doubting or not, the vet helped treat the starved kitty while the Whitaker family and the movers waited in suspense. When they finally got some news, it was not good: the vet told them not to expect Tiger to live. Tiger's organs were too damaged to recover. "I'll put him on an IV for 24 hours," said the vet.

The next day, the Whitakers took Tiger home, prepared to dig his grave as soon as his time came, but it didn't take long to see that his health was improving. He had already begun to perk up.

They fed him again and again, and he devoured every bite, though he still struggled to keep it in his belly. But as the days progressed, Tiger's stomach returned to normal. Incredibly, within only six weeks, he was back up to 14 pounds, acting lively and cheeky as ever, just like the Tiger they always knew.

He became so healthy that he and his new girl-friend Stubbie soon gave the Whitakers' children a lesson in the birds and the bees. Only a few months after the Whitakers were told that Tiger wouldn't live, they had five little Tigers running around to mock the vet's expectations.

In his lifetime, Tiger traveled from Germany to Alabama, to army bases in Texas, Mississippi and Virginia, and then on to the Pentagon. Finally, he retired with Colonel Whitaker and Nancy on their Virginia farm.

The adventurous miracle cat could fill many chapters of this book. For the Whitakers, he became a bit of a local celebrity. The movers came to check up on Tiger from time to time, and he was always a subject of the Christmas cards the family received (even more than their children!). It was common to overhear co-workers talking about the cunning cat that smuggled his way to America. People even accused Nancy and her husband of hiding Tiger to save on airfare. She would always remind them that with the money they spent on vet bills, they could have flown him across the world if they had wanted.

Despite his ordeal, Tiger never changed his playboy ways. One girlfriend wasn't enough; he would often leave for days at a time. On one occasion, he took a 30-day holiday and had to be bailed out of the pound. Tiger thrived for 18 years before he died peacefully of natural causes in 2005.

"The morning he died," remembers Nancy, "I was getting ready to go to work. I went over by the door and looked at him. He was lying on his doormat. I turned my head for just a few seconds and when I looked back, he had stopped breathing." Nancy went upstairs and woke her husband, telling him, "It's time to go out and dig the grave."

But before they buried him, they waited. His body was still warm and eyes still open, and they weren't about to give up on him again, especially considering what he had pulled through. So they waited until they were sure he had gone. Now Tiger has his grave in their back yard.

As for the Whitakers' sons, they have followed in their parents' footsteps: they both joined the Air Force and are now captains with a set of cats that look exactly like Tiger and Stubbie.

Too Curious for Her Own Good
Peter Myers owns a popular British delicatessen in Greenwich Village, the heart of old New York. His business, Myers of Keswick, is inside a 157-year-old

brick building surrounded by structures from the same era that are legally considered historic landmarks. Because of the building's age, it is also a landmark for rodents. Peter keeps Molly, a black and white kitty, inside the deli to keep the pests in line.

One day in April 2006, Molly went missing. Between baking goods, serving customers and ringing in sales, Peter had little time to track down the cat. He figured she had to be around somewhere, and things would work themselves out eventually.

But they didn't. After several days, there was still no sign of Molly. Peter turned the place upside down looking for her, but to no avail. At best, he thought, she had run out of the building and found herself a new, loving home. At worst…well, he tried to push that thought out of his mind. He had a business to run and bills to pay, so life went on.

But several days after Molly went missing, sad meows could be heard on the other side of the brick wall of the deli. The staff wasn't positive that it was Molly, but it sure sounded a lot like her when she was hungry. Where the meows were coming from was a mystery. The wall didn't lead directly outdoors; it led to a narrow alley between two very old buildings, so narrow that only a cat could squeeze through it. And aside from the maze of bricks, pipes and beams, nobody could guess what else had accumulated between those walls over the century.

Regardless of the risks and possible bad outcome, a rescue mission was undertaken. Various animal rescuers, police officers, firefighters, nearby contractors and construction workers, bystanders and even customers contributed as much as they could to get Molly—or whatever cat it was—out safely. But there was only so much the rescuers could do. They couldn't just start breaking down walls and drilling holes, because the Landmarks Preservation Commission set a lot of limitations. The commission did, however, cooperate as much as possible and even supplied cat food with the hope that it could be used to cajole the cat from its hiding place. It didn't work, and neither did catnip.

Thinking that maybe Molly would respond to a maternal instinct, they brought two kittens to the alley, hoping she would be drawn to them. When that failed, it was pretty obvious that Molly was trapped and not just too stubborn to leave.

The rescue team slipped a wiry camera through the opening in the wall and looked around for her. It was just the first of many cameras at the scene.

The site attracted one local FOX News affiliate, which was shooting a segment that had more to do with the commission's troubles over the cat than with Molly herself. Once that aired, however, people recognized it as Molly's story. More and more media flocked to the scene of the cat crisis. Camera crews from ABC, CBS and NBC were filming from all angles, and then the logos on the

reporters' microphones became more unfamiliar—
the international media had arrived. This naturally
attracted bystanders, who then became customers
in the deli, which in turn increased Peter's business. It was chaotic. At any given moment during
the longstanding rescue, there were up to 50
observers, all of whom had an opinion about how
to save Molly. And the advice ranged from the
improbable to the downright delusional.

One person claiming to be a cat psychic and
therapist believed that they could track down
Molly using astrology. All they needed was the
cat's horoscope. Another observer suggested they
sing to Molly and let the melody move her body to
freedom. Someone recommended they get a ferret
in there, because, naturally, Molly would chase
the ferret outside.

Another individual suggested the cat food they
were using was the reason Molly was still
trapped. Apparently, American cat food wouldn't
cut it—what they needed was French cuisine!
As they say, "Only in New York." The serious rescuers called it the "Here, Kitty, Kitty Mentality,"
because the eager helpers couldn't get it through
their heads that the cat was trapped, not lost, and
not lounging around. The situation was so out of
control that a suggestion box was set up for all the
ideas. It was cleverly placed 10 blocks away from
the site, but that didn't keep the area clean of

gung-ho volunteers, whom the rescue team could have done without.

After exhausting all their options, the last alternative chosen was to go through the wall, not the alley; because there was so much elevated garbage accumulated between the brick buildings, any sudden intrusion could cause them to collapse and suffocate Molly. Peter Myers was hesitant to break down his walls, but he understood that it was the only way to rescue the cat. And besides, after two weeks of non-stop efforts, he could just not give up.

With hammers and drills, they beat out three layers of brick from the deli's basement. Finally, a tunnel-worker-turned-volunteer, Kevin Clifford, shimmied his way through the hole and found what they were looking for. It was Molly all right—dirty, scared and skinny, trapped between a sheet of metal, a brick wall and century-old trash. Kevin reached in, only able to grab hold of her leg, and pulled the screaming, scrambling kitty out.

It took exactly two weeks to save Molly, and only a few minutes to get her a bowl of her favorite dish: sardines and pork roast. In no time, she returned to her duty of pest control.

Cat-toid

In 2003, Americans purchased $3.4 billion worth of food for their feline friends.

When Harry Met Sally

Heart murmurs in humans usually signify hardship to come, but in kittens, a heart murmur is not uncommon. In basic checkups, vets regularly examine cats for abnormal heart sounds, and if a murmur is detected, it's usually insignificant. When Sally and Terry Dolan had their three-month-old kitten Harry checked by a veterinarian, they learned that their new bundle of joy had a defective heart. They were told not to worry, but to be safe, the vet referred them to a cardiologist at Queen Mother Hospital for Animals.

Radiographs and ultrasounds at Queen Mother revealed that Harry had a double-chambered right ventricle, a very rare condition in which the location of hypertrophied muscular bands is abnormal. Sally and Terry returned home relieved because there was no evidence of heart failure. Not yet, anyway. But just in case, Harry's owners purchased pet health care from a company called PetPlan. For just over $30 per month, Harry was insured.

It was a smart move that paid off greatly a few months later.

Harry was having trouble breathing and seemed fatigued. Recognizing the signs, the Dolans returned him to his vet. His condition had caused a major build-up of fluids in his chest, which was drained with a needle, and he was treated with medication. But the medicine could not protect him from the inevitable. Harry was given 12 to 18 months to live, or he could be euthanized earlier. The only other option—one that was expensive and risky and had not proven to be successful in a cat before—was heart surgery.

Many dogs have had their hearts under the knife and have lived to bark about it. But cats have smaller bodies with much smaller hearts pumping much less blood. Before Harry, heart surgery on cats had been attempted, but always with grim results. Harry's chance at survival was low.

The Dolans decided to play it day by day.

Months later, Harry collapsed without warning. The couple discussed their options with the Queen Mother cardiology tcam, but there wasn't much time to think it over. Knowing that Harry would probably die if nothing were done, the Dolans decided that heart surgery was the only choice left, and besides, he was insured. Sally and Terry gave the go-ahead for the surgery.

The big day came, and the innovative operation was documented in a two-episode BBC show called *Super Vets*.

The hospital staff and the Dolans were astonished by Harry's quick recovery. In fact, he recovered so well that he was a bit of a handful for Queen Mother workers, so they sent him home to cool off.

But the recovery wasn't without complications.

Harry's health started to deteriorate again. Just like his condition before the surgery, Harry was short of breath. He was rushed back to Queen Mother. Thankfully, all that was needed this time was another fluid draining. And another. And another. Nothing can be done to prevent fluids from building up in Harry's chest, but the doctors' and assistants' hard work in strengthening his heart should be enough to keep him going, so long as he is checked regularly.

The approximate cost of the operation was £11,000 ($21,500) all paid for—every pound and penny—by PetPlan. The Dolans were happy with their decision to insure Harry, but they're probably happier that they adopted him in the first place.

His fight for survival, from kitten to cat, touched the hearts of millions who watched it unfold on TV. His surgery, and subsequent recovery, was a medical breakthrough; for Sally, however, it was just about doing the right thing for a living, loving creature.

~❦~

Cat-toid

Cats don't have taste buds that can detect sweetness in foods.

CHAPTER THREE

Motherly Meows

ANY PARENT WILL TELL YOU that raising a child is one of the hardest things to do, but for single mothers, it is especially difficult. In Canada, 15 percent of households are headed by a single mother. But in the cat world, that percentage is much higher, probably closer to 99 percent. If cats could speak, they'd probably say they've got it much harder.

Cats, when not domesticated and housed, live in communal environments without a male role model. It's not that the boyfriends and fathers are irresponsible party animals, running around and trying to get as many kitty phone numbers as possible; it's simply biology. The male's role is to breed, and the female's role is to raise the offspring. If you see a group of cats, the adults will probably be females with a litter of mixed gender kittens. The mothers usually rear their own kittens but often get help from the other adult females. It's important, however, that the mothers favor their own kittens because kittens learn best from their real mums.

A study at New York Medical College found that kittens sitting in on lessons from their mothers learned much faster than kittens in a class with

The protectiveness of mother cats can mean the difference between life and death for kittens.

~◦✕◦~

unrelated female teachers. The researchers set up a lever-operated food dispenser and trained two groups, one of mother cats and the other a group of cats with no kittens, to use it. Then they brought in the kittens. Not surprisingly, the kittens observing the acts of a strange cat struggled to pick up on the mechanics of the food dispenser. Although both groups were on par by the next day, in the real world time is crucial. One day could be the difference between life and death.

The study also proved something else; a surrogate mother cat is better than none at all. A third group, which served as a control group, was added to the experiment. Kittens in the control group had no mother figure and were forced to rely solely on trial and error. The kittens never figured out how to operate the lever and without the intervention of researchers would have starved.

But as is the case with humans, it's important that the mother cats give their kittens the rites of passage and eventually treat them like adults. An experiment at Chicago Institute for Psychoanalysis discovered that six-week-old kittens given a saucer of milk when they were ready to detach from their mothers' nipples were more organized and goal-driven and less fearful overall than kittens forced to nurse from their mothers until they were 12 weeks old.

A third group of kittens were removed from their mothers at only two weeks old, and this proved to be too early. These kittens were not only disorganized and fearful, but they also were slower to recover from the weaning process and some even developed chronic illnesses.

Obviously, it's vital for a kitten to have a support-
ive mother for as long as it needs one, until it
reaches adulthood. But something else happens as
a kitten ages. As it grows bigger and wiser, becomes
more self-sufficient and, of course, learns to defend
itself, the mother's predatory skills decrease. It is
almost an exchange of protective instincts, with
the kitten seeming to suggest to its mother, "Don't
worry, Mom. I can take it from here."

But until a kitten comes of age, it is very dependent on its mother, and for a good reason. When
this unpredictable world weighs down on them,
it's up to super-moms, like Scarlett in the next
story, to keep these kittens alive.

Scarlett: Hero, Mother and Media Darling

March 1996 seemed like a morbid month no
matter what news source you consulted. A Scottish
gunman killed 16 primary school students, the
bloody Menendez Brothers trial was soaking up
front pages and a violent standoff between police
and a grassroots militia erupted in Montana.
Adding to the atmosphere, a strain of mad cow
disease had just been discovered in humans. But
for a brief time, in the last days of the month,
an inspirational story commandeered the media.

A condemned garage in a seedy part of Brooklyn,
New York, caught fire, possibly because of arson,
though even today the cause is unclear. What caused
the fire seemed irrelevant, however, compared to

the incredible kitten survivors and their daring mother.

Scarlett lived in the desolate garage with her five four-week-old babies, and like most cat moms, she was a single mother. The lone parent may not have been the first to awake from the blaze, but she was the only one able to react in a lifesaving manner.

Pragmatically, she attended the kittens one by one. Scarlett bit into the back of their fleshy necks, and carried them out of the garage, away from the smoke and flames. With each trip inside, the obstacles worsened. The fire grew larger; the floor, hotter; the smoke, thicker. Each time she entered the building, it was like descending into another level of hell.

By the time she had all five babies safely outside the building, Scarlett was almost completely singed, her skin severely burned and bloody. Her ears were disfigured and her eyes blistered shut. Her lungs were filled with toxic fumes, and yet Scarlett wasn't finished.

Realizing that the blaze was burgeoning and she and her kittens were still in danger, she made another round of trips, this time taking her babies across the street to where it was safer. One by one, she pulled them up with her teeth. She only managed to transfer three of the five before collapsing next to them.

David Gianelli, a 17-year veteran firefighter, found her lying unconscious by three meowing kitties across the street from the blaze. He heard more cries near the fire and found the other two kittens. He gathered all six cats into a box to take them to North Shore Animal League (NSAL) in Long Island, where 10 years earlier, he had dropped off a badly burned dog. As he carried the box away, he noticed that Scarlett had regained consciousness. He observed her touching each kitten with the tip of her nose. David realized that Scarlett was conducting a head-count. She was using her nose because the fire and smoke had rendered her eyes useless.

When news of Scarlett's courageous display of maternal love was first reported, it broke the monotonous horror that was consuming the air-waves at the time. Her story touched people across the world, and when word got out that she was in need of a home, thousands of adoption offers poured into NSAL's office by phone and mail. Countless cards, letters, poems and written prayers flooded their mailbox. (Not to mention the unknowable number of silent prayers reserved for her across the globe.)

The kittens, too, were getting a wave of adop-tion offers, but sadly, the number of kittens up for adoption went from five to four. After a month of treatment, a cloud-white kitten died from smoke inhalation. The other four, however, rehabilitated fully, and in time were adopted.

Debbie Palmarozzo took "Smokey" and "Oreo" into her Long Island home, and Corinne and Ginette Vercillo, also Long Island residents, took home "Samsara" and "Panuki."

That left Scarlett. After three months of surgery and rehab to regain her vision, she was ready for a human companion. Workers at NSAL couldn't decide who the best owner would be, and they certainly wanted the best home for Scarlett, so they held an essay-writing contest. Anyone serious about adopting her had to write a convincing essay explaining why they were the most suitable. Hoping this would trim the number of applicants, NSAL workers were surprised to receive over 2000 essays.

After an exhausting search, they found an appropriate owner. A person that needed Scarlett as much as Scarlett needed her. A person that, like Scarlett, had suffered terrible injuries in an accident and needed healing companionship.

Seven years earlier, Karen Wellen was in a life-changing car accident. As she recovered at home, she was met with another tragedy—her cat died. Bringing Scarlett into her home was truly therapeutic. Not only would Scarlett fill the void left by

Cat-toid

Female cats can conceive a litter through "superfecundation," which means kittens in the same litter can have different fathers.

the passing of Karen's cat, but the pair could cope with their injuries together.

Today, Scarlett is a healthy 16 pounds. Her face is mostly hairless, but the rest of her body sports a luscious coat. Three times a day, ointment is applied to her eyes, which are scarred but tell an incredible story. And if those eyes don't say enough, then you can refer to the two books she inspired, the episode of *Sally Jessy Raphael* and PBS documentary she appeared in, or the thousands of articles written about her over the last 12 years. Truly, she is unforgettable.

A Faithful Feline

Faith first came to St. Augustine's Church in 1936 as a persistent stray who ignored the verger's demands that she shoo away and never come back. After her repeated attempts to take shelter in the warm church, Father Henry Ross finally let her stay. He had the verger's wife fix up an area of the church for her, with a bowl to eat from and a box to sleep in. It was supposed to be a temporary stay until her owner claimed her. By the time it was realized that she didn't have an owner—or did and was abandoned because of the Great Depression—Faith had already become a big hit at the church. So she stayed.

Aside from her superb mousing skills, Faith was also a wonderful comforter, alleviating the congregation's hardships through to the end of the Dirty Thirties and the beginning of World

War II. Two altar-guild women named Ruth and Clara had a special fondness for Faith, and they assisted Father Ross in caring for her when his guidance was needed elsewhere.

Four years into her stay, Faith seemed to be getting exceptionally chubby. Neither Father Ross nor the altar-guild women were spoiling her with food because, after all, the country was still in the Great Depression and war was looming over Great Britain. Even if they wanted to feed her that extra meal, they couldn't afford it. But before long, it all made sense. In Faith's little designated sleeping box, the staff found a lone kitten, which they named Panda. Rather than find another home for Panda, they let nature take its course, and Faith looked after him like any loving mother cat would.

In early September 1940, Father Ross noticed Faith acting especially strange. She meowed desperately for his attention as he sat at his desk. After she finally convinced him to rise, she led him out of his office, through the church and downstairs to the basement door. She continued barraging him with meows, until he opened the door to the dark, dusty storage room containing old books and music notes.

On his return to his office, he noticed Faith carrying Panda by the scruff of his little neck, carrying him from the box to the basement. Father Ross ignored it. But when she never returned the kitten to his sleeping box, he worried for the little one's health in that filthy room. *Who knows what's in that room?* he thought. *There are probably rats bigger than him that would eat him alive.*

So Father Ross descended to the basement, carefully picked up Panda and returned him to the box. But that wasn't the end of it for Faith.

For two days straight, Faith smuggled her son to the storage room, and Father Ross brought Panda back upstairs and put him in the box. However, Faith was as persistent now as she had been four years earlier when she was searching for a home. Under the advice of Ruth and Clara, who convinced him that mother knows best, Father Ross let the cats stay in the basement.

On the night of September 9, 1940, Father Ross was out of London seeking assistance for his ravaged neighborhood. Just two days earlier, a German blitzkrieg tore apart the street where his church was located. Despite the air raid sirens, 400 people were killed. Luckily, he survived, as did his church, but he feared a repeat.

While he was riding his bike home from Westminster, the air sirens began screeching for a second time. He immediately took refuge in a shelter, turned on the radio and listened. It was reported that eight London churches were destroyed in the battle. When the blitzkrieg was over and it was safe to leave the shelter, Father Ross rushed to St. Augustine's Church, only to find it in a heap of smoldering wood, brick and ash. He introduced himself to an emergency crew on scene, telling them that the church cats were trapped inside. He begged for their help in retrieving them.

The emergency aides didn't mean to insult Father Ross, but the honest truth was that they couldn't be bothered saving feline casualties when the number of possible human casualties was so high. But Father Ross was undeterred. He started his one-man rescue mission to retrieve Faith and Panda from the debris.

Although the true story of how he found and saved the cats will never be known, people say that Father Ross courageously climbed onto the hot rubble and began scouring the wreckage for an opening to the basement. Somehow he found his way in and began calling Faith's name until he thought he heard a meow. He followed what his ears or imagination had heard. In between clawing his way through the piles of paper, he looked up to see an increasingly unstable roof fighting against the weight of the debris. But he stayed as persistent as Faith would, calling her name and listening for her voice.

And then he found the cats.

Cat-toid

Over a seven-year period, two felines and their offspring can reproduce as many as 420,000 cats.

Fighting against time, he scooped them up and made a run for it. Rumor has it that as soon as he emerged from the wreckage, the basement roof finally collapsed. The cats would surely have been killed had they been below it.

Faith and Panda stayed with the verger and his wife in their home, but they always went to St. Augustine's site with Father Ross and the verger as the men worked diligently to rebuild the church. When it was finally reconstructed, the cats went home where they belonged. Faith lived and died in that church.

In 1948, she passed away peacefully in her sleep. The next morning, St. Augustine's Church was packed with well-wishers. The congregation held a mourning service for the cat. Faith was placed in a wooden box, blessed and then carried to the church cemetery to be buried with the others in her congregation.

A Symbol of Hope or a Hoax?

Sixty years after Faith and Panda were rescued from the German blitzkrieg, a similar story occurred halfway across the globe in a very different war. But as you will read, the truth behind the story is not known.

The last human survivors of the collapsed Twin Towers were found in 24 hours. By October 17, the pieces were still smoldering, and it would continue for 63 more days, but on that fateful morning, rescue workers found another group of survivors. Creatures so small, they survived by taking shelter inside a small box amid the rubble.

The owner of a basement restaurant that once served World Trade Center workers on their lunch break was searching the debris for anything salvageable. What he found was a gray cat, emaciated and weak, along with her three kittens, all nestled in a tissue container.

The cats were immediately taken to the Brooklyn Center for Animal Care and Control, where Dr. John Charros treated them. The mother was very sick with the flu. In Dr. Charros' care, she returned to good health and regained the five pounds she'd lost while trapped in Ground Zero.

Workers at the animal center did manage to find homes for all four cats, but not before naming them. Appropriately, the kittens were christened "Amber," "Flag" and "Freedom." Their mother was christened "Hope."

Because they were so young and desperately needed proper nourishment, something their mother could not fully provide, Flag and Freedom died before meeting their adoptive parents. Amber, however, is now a healthy seven-year-old.

The story of the cats reached the press at a time when Americans were still grieving for their casualties, and the death toll was not holding still. American-led troops were 10 days into a war with a strange and complex enemy, and it was already proving more difficult than first imagined. Some skeptics believe the Hope story was exaggerated to boost national morale at a time when good news was scarce but badly needed.

Myth-busters Barbara and David P. Mikkelson of Snopes.com—the most widely used urban legend debunking archive—say that there are insufficient sources to prove that the cats didn't just wander in after the collapse. Also, only a small TV news crew in Minnesota broke the story; it seems strange that the uplifting report slipped past all major media, especially when another cat, Precious (see Chapter 2), was reported on extensively by international press only three weeks earlier.

A representative of the Brooklyn Center for Animal Care and Control said that the kittens were less than three weeks old when they were found. That means they were born two weeks after the towers collapsed. Kittens that young would have the strength and vision to follow their mother into a tissue box, but they would be very bad at it, and rescue workers would have most likely spotted them.

As improbable as the alternative is, it is possible that Hope was pregnant and had her children in the disaster zone under much strife. It is possible for cats to endure weeks, even months, in tough conditions. Felines are gifted when it comes to survival. The smallest drop of water can mean the difference between life and death, and there was plenty of September rain for the cats to drink in the cramped container. As for nourishment, maybe Hope found food in her surroundings; the cats were trapped in a restaurant, after all. But would the food be edible considering the air itself was toxic?

There were other rumors surrounding the September 11 attacks that were used to boost spirits but later proved false. A fabricated story about an unscathed Bible that was found in the pieces of the Pentagon restored people's faith, and, Hope's story, whether it was real or not, helped restore their faith, too. But whether she and her kittens actually survived the collapse of the towers is relevant to the emotional response the story received. Hope's story is, at the very least, true in that the Ground Zero rescuers and volunteers never gave up, ever.

Cat Food or Cat Family?

In some Middle Eastern towns, it is common to see a merchant, usually a little boy or girl no older than 10, strolling through the quarters, selling chicks out of a cardboard box. When I say "chicks," I don't mean chicken and I don't mean eggs. The little traders sell newly born chicks in a variety of colors.

It's an unusual sight to look inside the box and see bright green, pink and blue birds bouncing up

Cat-toid

The Guinness record for most kittens born in one litter is 19.

and down, peeping their little beaks off. They are such unnatural colors because they've been dyed that way. It is no doubt cruel, but the life span of these tortured creatures is even more unkind.

When I was seven years old, I bought two chicks, one pink and one blue, from a Lebanese vendor my age and size. I paid a total of 25 cents for the pair, and within 24 hours, they were dead. One of the many feral cats got into their shoebox home and gobbled them up. It's no surprise; cats kill about 100 million birds a year. Killer cats are third only to killer electricity lines and glass windows in causing bird deaths.

But sometimes, a cat's maternal instincts are stronger than its predatory instincts.

Take, for instance, Nimra, a one-year-old Jordanian house cat who took seven wild-colored chicks under her paw. And not only was Nimra blind to the difference in species and fur color, she was also impartial to size. While her own four kittens frolicked around her and then rested from their play to nurse, the chicks played their games, too, and although they couldn't feed from Nimra, they snuggled up to the cat as though they were her biological kittens.

Nimra wasn't just being civil by not eating the chicks or by letting them loiter in her cardboard home. She actually took care of the chicks. When a chick wandered too far from the family, Nimra fol-lowed the bird, picked it up with her teeth—without swallowing it—took it back to the box, plopped it down with its "siblings" and kept a watchful eye in case that chick decided to make another run for it. Her special protection allowed the chicks to grow and their feathers to finally return to their natural gold tone.

A mother cat's innate desire to care for and love can transcend all instincts. Sometimes, like Nimra, cats see no difference between baby felines and other babies. If their hearts are big enough, they can become surrogate mothers to just about any needy animal, even their eternal nemesis—the dog.

Surrogate Moms

Smoochy the cocker spaniel gave birth to a litter of pups, but she wasn't quite ready for motherhood. She neglected the puppies from the start, as if they didn't come from her loins at all. Although it's unusual for mother dogs to be so negligent, Smoochy had a reputation for being noncommittal. The farm dog was either inside the house or leashed to a tree outside, because, without restraint, she was keen to escape.

Around the same time that Smoochy abandoned her pups, her orange tabby stepsister, Miss Kitty, gave birth to a litter of kittens, but none of them survived. Whether it was an act of confusion, maternal instinct or "pup-itarianism," Miss Kitty took the puppies in as her own offspring.

She carried each pup with her mouth to her special trailer home and welcomed all six into the family. There, she nursed them, a delicate sight of six black pooches swarming the belly of the golden, nonchalant cat.

The unusual family lives on Missy Grant's farm in South Carolina. Missy admits that the cat's behavior is odd, but she was just happy to see the puppies get a good upbringing and have a positive role model for the future. Hopefully, when the puppies reach adolescence, they won't forget who raised them, cared for them and taught them how to purr. But as most mothers know, a rebellious phase is almost always inevitable.

❧◆☙

Susie Mason works at a Californian diner in the town of Murrieta. One day in April 2007 when she was at work—thinking about her cat Tinkerbell's new litter of three kittens born the night before—she overheard her co-worker Connie conversing on the phone about her Chihuahua's reluctant motherhood. She eavesdropped on Connie's dilemma: "There are three of them....No, she won't take care of them, won't nurse them at all...I don't know what to do."

Susie had an idea. Instead of bottle-feeding the puppies, as Connie was doing at the time, she thought it would be better to put the pups in with Tinkerbell and her kittens. That way they could get proper nourishment from Tinkerbell's milk. Neither woman thought it would work, but they figured it was worth trying because any animal that's not parented immediately after birth is critically endangered.

They decided to give the experiment a day to see if it would work. As it turned out, they needed only a few hours. By the evening of that same day, Tinkerbell was nursing the brown and white Chihuahua puppies even though they were a different color and much smaller than her kittens. All that mattered to Tinkerbell was that they were healthy and safe.

But after the sibling puppies and kitties were all grown up, they had to be separated. To ease the split, Susie adopted one of the pups, and Connie, one of the kittens.

~❦~

Cat-toid

According to a study by researchers at the University of Alberta, cats learn best from acting, not observing. Visual cues may be enough for retaining short-term memories, but for long-term memories, they must learn from physical practices. They are kinesthetic learners.

CHAPTER FOUR

Whiskers of War

IN 500 BCE, PERSIA WAS near defeat in their war with Egypt, until the Persian army general devised a plan that involved cats. Knowing that Egyptian culture believed cats to be sacred, the general had his men round up as many cats as they could. They then entered the eastern Egyptian town of Pelusium and released the cats. Egyptians were dumbfounded by the felines scurrying about on the battlefield. They wouldn't dare harm the sacred animals, and they surrendered.

Another legend says that the Persian army used cats as shields to thwart the Egyptians. Again, Persia's enemies wouldn't dare put a single blade through the felines, dead or alive—it was sacrilegious.

If these legends are true, then part of the reason the Persians won the war was their cruel, but cunning, use of cats, and they set a precedent for using helpless cats during wartime.

During World War I, the British used felines as poison detectors. Before entering a battlefield, they gave the cats a head start and monitored their survival. If the felines showed signs of weakness or, more likely, dropped dead, the British retreated.

In World War II, a Russian cat named Mourka became something of a hero. During the 1942 siege of Stalingrad, she was used to carry messages across a dangerous street.

But the cruelest abuse of cats in war was actually during a war in which not a single bullet was fired. At the peak of the Cold War, the United States Central Intelligence Agency (CIA) had just about exhausted every spying technique they could think of to use on the Communists. The mind-controlling tests failed. The psychics they hired materialized a whole lot of nothing. The exploding or poisonous cigars sent to Fidel Castro were never lit. What more could the CIA try? They took a page from the Persian battle book and resorted to cats.

Operation Acoustic Kitty was a six-year espionage experiment kept top secret until it was declassified with 40 other CIA Science and Technology Directorate files in 2006. It involved spies, microphones, Soviets and one very unfortunate cat.

Forty-odd years ago, the CIA had an almost limitless budget. Whatever crazy scheme an officer came up with would get approved, as long it worked in theory. So when some genius proposed a plan to insert a microphone inside a cat and train it to lurk around potential spies, the government handed over $25 million to give it a shot.

They brought a cat into their lab, slit it open as much as they could without killing the poor thing and inserted a microphone and batteries. They also slipped an antenna into the tail to raise frequency levels. Former CIA officer Victor Marchetti described it to the press as "a monstrosity."

Several tests were performed on the cat. Over and over again, researchers found that the cat wasn't as docile as they had expected. During the course of completely stripping him of any soul or sense of life, they seemed to have forgotten that the cat was actually a living creature and would therefore require food occasionally. Somehow the CIA was surprised when the cat continuously wandered off the job to quell his hunger. Well, instead of feeding it, they just operated again, this time implanting a wire that eliminated the cat's appetite.

"They took [the cat] out to a park bench and said, 'Listen to those two guys. Don't listen to anything else—not the birds, no cat or dog—just those two guys,'" recalls Marchetti. The park bench, he remembers, was across from the Soviet compound on Wisconsin Avenue in Washington, DC.

The cat was ready for his first test. Officers drove him in a van, parked across the street and let him out. The potential spies were only yards away. Soon they'd be exchanging super-secret dialogue, probably one of them saying to the other, "Hey, it's just me, you, these classified plans of ours and this

Black cats are not strangers to war; during the Middle Ages they were slaughtered because of their rumored association with the devil.

inconspicuous cat with a metallic tail rubbing up against my leg. Let's get to business."

Well, their efforts didn't make it that far, because someone must have forgotten to implant a chip in the cat that taught it to look both ways before crossing the street. As soon as he stepped onto the road, a taxi smoked him. (To this day, it's unsure whether the taxi driver is now or has ever been a member of the Communist Party.)

And that was it. After six years of experiments and a lottery-sized budget, the CIA trashed their plans and moved on to whatever nutty notions they thought of next. However, before they called it quits, they sent someone to the accident site to gather the cat's remains. They kept the kitty in a private place where the Soviets would never find him. If the Soviets had uncovered the remains, they would probably have realized their enemies weren't worth spying on anyway, perhaps ending the Cold War 25 years earlier.

Fortunately, not every whisker on the war front is a sad one. Sometimes these cats find themselves caught up in the tragedies of warfare, only to become heroes and inspirations to the creatures that created the conflict.

Captain Simon

For centuries, humans in the line of fire have been recognized for their courage. When a Canadian or British soldier displays self-sacrifice or commendable bravery in the face of an enemy, he or she is awarded with the Victoria Cross. American soldiers who save the life of a comrade receive a Purple Heart. In Ancient Rome, when an army general made a command that was believed to have saved the legion, he was decorated with the Grass Crown. But what about the animals on the battlefront? What do they get for their sacrifices? An animal on active service for any free country is eligible for the Dickin Medal.

The Dickin Medal is the creation of the People's Dispensary for Sick Animals (PDSA) founder, Maria Dickin. During World War II, she found inspiration in the birds and horses giving their lives for the liberation of the United Kingdom. She started the Armed Forces Mascot Club (AFMC) to recognize these furry and feathered heroes. The award, a big bronze medal, has the words "For Gallantry" and "We Also Serve" engraved on it. Since 1943, 60 animals have been recognized for their gallantry: 32 pigeons, 24 dogs, three horses and one cat. Only one cat? How did rodents with wings get more prestige than gods with whiskers? (Whatever; at least one medal is more than gerbils were ever awarded.)

The lone recipient was Simon, an all-black cat known to his comrades as Blackie. Simon was discovered in 1948, just two years after the end of the war, but still a shaky time for the planet, especially in the Asian Pacific.

At a dockyard in Hong Kong, a young man named George Hickinbottom, just 17 years old, found Simon, 16 years his junior, on Stonecutters Island. George was a seaman on the Royal Navy's HMS *Amethyst*, which was set to sail to Nanjing along the Yangtze River to guard China's British Embassy during the Chinese Civil War. The ship docked in Hong Kong for supplies. Nowhere on the supply list did it say "one black cat." But George adored Simon and refused to leave him behind. Because of his young age, George was probably hungry for companionship on the ship. He picked Simon up, cradled him in his arms and then slipped him under his tunic. He smuggled the cat

into his space, which was smaller than the rest of
the cabins, and made sure the cat stayed inside at
all times. He couldn't let the strict captain find the
feline and, George probably imagined, throw him
overboard.

George obviously didn't know the captain too
well. Lieutenant Commander Ian Griffiths happened
to be an ailurophile and even had cats back home
with his wife and children. When the captain discovered Simon, he wasn't a bit irked. He simply
told George that as long as Simon didn't defecate
on board (though I'm sure his language was more
colorful), he could stay on as their ratter.

And it just so happens that Simon was a bit of
a "captain-ophile." If he wasn't sleeping, he was
following Griffiths everywhere. When Simon
was asleep, usually in the captain's cap in his
cabin, Griffiths need only blow his whistle and
Simon would heed his call. Simon must have
sensed Griffith's power and authority because he
always tried to impress his commander, leaving
rodents at Griffith's feet or on his bed. Griffiths
probably appreciated the former gesture more. But
the man and cat's friendship soon came to an end.
Griffiths was transferred, and in came Captain
Skinner to replace him.

Skinner also was a cat man, but he lacked the
aura of authority that Griffiths possessed. Simon
seemed to be aware of this, and he never followed
Skinner anywhere and never responded to his

whistle. However, Simon did find solace in the captain's cabin, and he wasn't giving that up for anybody—captain or not.

Despite his snootiness to one very important fellow, Simon was appreciated by the rest of the seamen on board. The cat's carefree presence provided a distraction during the tense war. Every day, the seamen heard bombshells explode, but they could hardly tell who was firing what and which side, if any, was winning. The Brits hadn't yet taken sides in the Chinese Revolution, but on April 20, 1949—when all those audible bombs suddenly became visual—they were forced to choose.

The first 10 shells fired at the *Amethyst* missed. The crewmen on board were startled, but they assumed it was stray fire. The ship sped up and unfurled Union flags to prevent deadly consequences to a case of mistaken identity. It worked...but only for one hour.

When the next battery opened fire, the *Amethyst* took shots to her bridge and wheelhouse. And then there were more shots, more damage. While Simon was asleep in the captain's cabin, a shell landed in the space. Shrapnel caught Simon in the leg and back, but he survived. Sadly, Captain Skinner wasn't so lucky. After nearly two hours of shelling, 25 men, including Skinner, were dead or dying. More were injured.

Dehydrated, wounded, weak, partially singed and definitely traumatized, Simon managed to climb up to the deck. He saw the carnage, heard the wailing and stepped through the blood and shrapnel. The wounded men were moved to the sick bay, and Simon followed, perhaps sensing it was where help would be provided. He then crouched in a safe place and awaited treatment. The lone medical officer treated the seamen several at a time. When he had finished with his human patients, he moved on to Simon, washing his wounds and stitching him up. Simon had a speedier recovery than did his shipmates.

The Royal Navy sent HMS *Consort* to the rescue, but she was fired upon, leaving three more men dead. The *Consort* retreated, leaving the *Amethyst* back in its vulnerable position. With Skinner gone and no outside help, Simon and the men took command from First Lieutenant Geoffrey Weston. Weston, too, was injured, but he managed to take control of the *Amethyst* and move her up the Yangtze River a safe distance. Once out of range, British Naval Attaché Lieutenant Commander John Simon Kerans came aboard and took command.

Soon, more help was on the way. Two Ships, the *Black Swan* and the *London*, approached the *Amethyst*, but they too were forced to retreat by the Chinese Communists. The standoff would not end unless the Brits met the Communists' demands and made a public admission of firing first. It was obvious that the Brits were in it for the long run. That's when Simon began his humanitarian work of consoling the casualties.

He spent much of his time in the sick bay. The medical officer understood the benefits of pet therapy, so he kept Simon around to purr and cuddle with the traumatized men. They found his company soothing and were inspired by Simon's own recovery. The cat's empathy helped strengthen them and lift them from their shocked state.

Simon helped in other ways, too. His ratting abilities reduced the rat infestation. One threat, nicknamed "Mao Tse-Tung" by the crew, was a particularly large rat. Mao was quick, too, always evading every attempt to catch him. The men never expected Simon to kill the vermin because Simon was still weak and the rat was practically his size. But when Simon and Mao finally had their standoff, Simon demonstrated that the *Amethyst* could prevail by demolishing the Commie rat in a quick swoop, scratch and bite. The crew promoted him to Able Seacat, the feline version of Able Seaman, the person who acts as watch-stander and ship protector. The title fit him very well.

But as weeks sailed by, food and water supplies withered, and not even Simon could help with that. The seamen had to get out or die. On July 30, 1949, day 101 of the crisis, the *Amethyst* made a daring escape to open seas. The 100-mile dash was not without danger. Almost immediately, the shelling started up again, causing more damage to the ship but not to the men on board. Once free, the *Amethyst* met with HMS *Concord*.

A special ceremony took place on deck. Cradled by a seaman who stood at attention with the officers and crew, Simon was awarded the *Amethyst* campaign ribbon while a citation was read. Simon had received his first war decoration.

Word got out that AFMC wanted to award Simon for his gallantry, and that was the beginning of his journey to the Dickin Medal. The ceremony was set for December 11, 1949, about the same time the ship was to arrive in Britain, where Maria Dickin and the Lord Mayor of London were to award Simon the medal with a specially colored ribbon.

Tragically, as Simon's day neared, he contracted a virus and became sick. At every port, he was an international sensation, met with toys, food and poems, but none of it could strengthen him. He had exhausted his stamina and spirit. On the morning of November 28, just two weeks before the ceremony, Simon never awoke. The vet believed that he could have overcome the virus had he not been so weakened by the initial attack on the Yangtze River.

In a custom-made casket draped with the Union flag, Simon was buried with other Dickin medallists in the PDSA's animal cemetery. The obituaries of *Time* magazine also paid tribute to him.

Posthumously, Simon was awarded the Dickin Medal, and the following citation written by Lieutenant Commander John Simon Kerans was read:

Able Seaman Simon, for distinguished and meritorious service on HMS Amethyst, you are hereby awarded the Distinguished Amethyst Campaign Ribbon.

Be it known that on April 26, 1949, though recovering from wounds, when HMS Amethyst was standing by off Rose Bay, you did single-handedly and unarmed stalk down and destroy "Mao Tse Tung," a rat guilty of raiding food supplies which were critically short.

Be it further known that from April 22 to August 4 you did rid HMS Amethyst of pestilence and vermin, with unrelenting faithfulness.

Cat-toid

The parasite *Toxoplasma gondii* can only sexually reproduce inside a feline. When the parasite infects rats, it causes a brain malfunction that attracts the rodents to the scent of cat urine, instead of repelling them. Consequently, the rats crawl right into the cat's trap, which in turn falls right into the parasite's trap. The cat ingests the parasite, becomes infected and gives the parasite a place to reproduce.

Nine Lives, Three Ships, One Unlucky Cat

Oscar was a black cat in the truest sense; his remarkable penchant to bring bad luck to everything he put his paws on still baffles World War II historians. His wave of destruction began on the Nazi German battleship, *Bismarck*. He was a regular ship's cat, sailing the seas, dining on seafood and lounging about while the onboard fighters lived every day like it could be their last—until, one day, it was their last.

A British Royal Navy ship, HMS *Cossack*, torpedoed the *Bismarck* and blew her to smithereens. While most of the men aboard drowned, Oscar managed to pull himself out of the sea and onto a floating piece of wooden debris. When the *Cossack*'s admiral saw Oscar drifting on the flotsam, he sent his men to rescue the cat, and Oscar was made their official mascot.

The crew would not fully understand the jinx brought aboard with Oscar for another five months, but sure enough, the *Cossack* was sunk too. Oscar had to be rescued again. But he wasn't traded back to the Axis powers; instead, another British ship saved him.

The men aboard the aircraft carrier *Ark Royal* got an early glimpse of Oscar's recklessness when he was spotted carelessly walking the plank. The admiral put a stop to it, but only three weeks into the cat's post, a German U-boat torpedoed the

Ark Royal, and Oscar was back in the water, again stranded on flotsam.

Incredibly, the cat was pulled from the water for the third time in his life, this time by the *Ark Royal* admiral, though the seaman must surely have been aware of just how unlucky this cat was. Knowing that the Nazis would never be defeated so long as this cat was on duty, the admiral transferred Oscar to Belfast, England, where he stayed at a veterans home, The Home For Sailors, until he died of natural causes in 1955.

Vietnam Veteran

John Lawrence waited almost 40 years to write his book, *The Cat from Hue: A Vietnam War Story*. It's not clear why he held on to the story for so long, considering he knew the title almost immediately after meeting Meo in the late 1960s.

John was a war reporter working for CBS. He spent years covering Vietnam, sometimes independently and sometimes with the aid of U.S. marines.

One fateful day in 1968, he sat on the floor of a mortared house in Hue—a key battleground located mid-way between North and South Vietnam. Leaning his back against the wall, John shoveled food rations into his mouth. The marines were staked out in a house next door. John was alone; that is, until he got the first of two North Vietnamese visitors.

The first was a kitten. It stood in the doorway for a moment, eyeing John, perhaps debating whether he was a good or bad man, and whether he would stroke her or eat her. He did neither, and she, too, did nothing—just stood in the dark room, silhouetted by the light shining through a hole in the roof. After John finished his meal, he lit a cigarette, and the shutting of his lighter lid frightened the kitty. She scurried away.

John realized that in those brief minutes in the kitten's company, he had found a distraction from the gunfire and ominous blasts that sounded too near. He rose from the floor and walked out of the abandoned house in search of the kitten. He found her, balancing on a barrel rim and licking water off the surface. She was a calico cat, smaller than he thought—maybe eight weeks old. She was skeletal and covered in fleas. He wanted to pet her, despite her unhealthy appearance, but before he could, he found himself in the scope of a Vietcong enemy combatant.

John froze. The soldier had his gun ready and aimed at him. They gazed into each other's wide eyes for what probably felt like an era. And then—possibly because John was a media correspondent, or maybe because the soldier witnessed John's fondness of the kitten—the soldier lowered his gun, blinked his eyes, then turned and walked away.

When his heart started beating again, John re-entered the shelter and fell to the floor, his life flashing before his eyes. The cat followed him inside. John opened a can of rations for the cat, and the rest is history.

John named the kitten Meo, and she traveled with him through Vietnam and other war posts for 13 years. Her courage was noticed immediately; on the chopper ride out of Hue, she climbed onto the pilot's shoulder and watched the journey from her elevated point of view.

In the years during the Vietnam War, John kept her at the Saigon Continental Hotel, where she waited for him every night after work. It was all part of creating a home environment, an attempt to find stability and detach from violence. When he was away, the hotel staff looked after her, for a tip. The other journalists and friends who visited John at the Continental also welcomed the cat into their hearts. She was a small but significant source of escapism.

From Hue to Saigon, to John's mother's home in Connecticut, to his home in New York, and then finally to London with John and his wife, Meo grew into her once bony body, became a healthy adult and died of old age. Her legacy became literature in 2002.

Gods in Refuge

In the Middle East, where cats were first domesticated and where their virtues were first recognized, they face hardships like in no other place in the world. It is ironic: the region that first gave them the security of human companionship now threatens their safety because of human insecurity. During the Lebanese Civil War, hundreds of cats were abandoned by their owners, who fled to Europe, North America and safer Gulf countries. The human exodus resulted in a major influx of strays to the streets. To this day, the cat-human bond hasn't fully recovered to what it was during the pre-war days of domestication.

During my travels through Lebanon in the summer of 2007, I witnessed firsthand the community of stray and feral felines wandering the roads like hobos—taking refuge under cars, eating scraps from dumpsters and risking their lives to cross a road where traffic laws are considered mere suggestions. Almost every day, I experienced the same queasiness while stepping over another flattened casualty in a back alley.

When I did see a living kitten—usually bony and with fur so dirty it gave the cat the appearance of an earthworm—I'd want to pet it and take it into my apartment to share my lunch. But the threat of disease and attack from these wild creatures was too high. Instead, I spent my nights searching for sleep but was kept awake by the shrill yowling of fighting alpha male cats and the desperate cries of kittens, leaving me struggling between feeling sympathy and irritability.

The displaced-cats phenomenon is not unique to Lebanon, by any means. As war stretches through the region and spills across borders—from Lebanon to Palestine and Israel, to Iraq and Afghanistan—more cats become wild, untamable refugees. In a place where they were once symbolized as deities and vessels of gods, they have become devalued; they have become vermin.

⤳◆⤶

The year was 1991, and the Gulf War was seeping into Israel. A cat was alone in her Tel Aviv home, but only for the last few minutes. It wasn't long ago that her human companions were stroking her fur, filling her food dish and taunting her with a string and ball. But when the screeching siren exploded over the city, the cat's owners dashed in a panic, leaving their cat behind, scared and desperate. Suddenly the cat heard another whistle overhead, followed by a violent impact that brought the house down on it.

Although injured and deafened by the blast, the cat managed to rise from the ashes like the mythical phoenix. Hence, the cat was eventually named "Phoenix" by staff at the Cat Welfare Society of Israel (CWSI). But first, the cat needed to find safety. Phoenix climbed over the debris and wandered the desolate Tel Aviv streets.

Eventually Phoenix was discovered, like many other forgotten cats, and placed with the CWSI near the town of Tira. There, she was fed and looked after by Arabs and Jews working together to rescue the forgotten feline casualties of war.

What had made this once loved cat now homeless was an Iraqi Scud missile. Phoenix's story was reported in the May 2003 issue of *Cat Fancy*, when Phoenix's savior, Anne Moss of the CWSI, was interviewed while preparing for another season of rescuing cats, this time abandoned because of the new Iraq war.

⚜

At an American military base in the Sunni Triangle north of Baghdad, the soldiers often reported back from a mission drained and stressed. The anger of losing one of their cohorts, or coming so close to losing their own lives, had them banging on walls and shouting desperately to anyone in ear shot. The only stress relief they had was a striped Egyptian Mau that came to them on four legs to comfort them.

Hammer was born near the base, along with two siblings who ran away and dodged the frequent attacks. Hammer stayed behind to snuff out mice. When a mortar attack threatened his life, a soldier grabbed Hammer and put him under his body armor, waiting for the firing to cease. When it was all over, he brought Hammer inside the base, where the cat became the company's mascot.

Hammer's companions put one of the flea collars they tied around their ankles to fight sand fleas around his neck and hooked to it an army tag. He became Private First Class Hammer—a mouser, therapist and fellow soldier.

But in January 2004, Staff Sergeant Rick Bousfield was informed that his unit was headed home in three months. Of course, he and the other soldiers were elated, but he couldn't help feeling sorry for Hammer. *What will happen to him if he's left alone?* wondered Bousfield. He immediately began making arrangements to ship Hammer to America with the rest of the unit.

He emailed two organizations, the Alley Cat Allies (ACA) and Military Mascots, and asked for their help. The ACA began fundraising online to pay for Hammer's rescue, while Military Mascots handled the paperwork and transportation. Incredibly, it would cost thousands of dollars to get Hammer to the U.S., but more amazing was the number of people willing to donate money to get the kitty out of the crossfire.

At a cost of $2500, Hammer was neutered, inoculated and flown to America one week after

Cat-toid

Tabby cats are so named because their coats resemble an ancient silk that originated in a part of Baghdad called Attabiyah.

Bousfield arrived home in Fort Carson, Colorado. Hammer currently lives with Bousfield's family and five other cats in a permanently green zone free of bombs and bullets. But not even cats are immune to post-traumatic stress disorder. During thunderstorms, Hammer cowers, mistaking the explosions in the clouds for the ones he used to hear on the base.

Hammer is one of many animal soldiers rescued by Military Mascots. It seems that no matter which country or village American men and women are stationed in, the organization finds orphaned animals desperately in need of help. The cats and dogs that wander into their hearts are often used as counselors to help the soldiers cope in war-torn environments. But when the soldiers eventually come home, it's understandably hard to leave their four-footed friends behind.

Military Mascots takes requests, and with the donations of their supporters, makes arrangements with overseas veterinarians to inoculate the animals and ready them for a new American environment.

~❊~

CHAPTER FIVE

Traveling Tails

WHEN I TOLD MY DAD that I was writing this book, his usual stoicism vanished. "You should talk to me," he said. "I have many, many stories about cats from the homeland."

My father's homeland is Lebanon. I've been there, and I've seen Lebanon's cats—they're wild and diseased and absolutely terrifying. Every night, they fight, make mad love with each other or just yowl for pure whimsy. I dreaded whatever tales my father had to offer. I stood against the wall while he sat, puffing on his hookah, telling stories of the cats he had owned and the cats his friends owned. He animated his childhood cat stories with the hookah smoke like the Cheshire cat in *Alice in Wonderland*. Each story was more gritty and morbid than the one before, and strangely, each story also made him giddier.

"Dad," I interrupted. "This is a supposed to be an uplifting book. Stories that make you smile, you know. Not stories to make you queasy. I'm not going to write a book about cats losing their tails, jumping on spiked fences, or any of that stuff.

Don't you have any cat stories that involve, like, I don't know, them surviving?"

Dad exhaled and thought long and hard. He scratched his mustache, stopped, and held up his index finger, like an unspoken "Eureka!"

He told me about a time when he was 12 years old. He was the eldest son of a poor family that was growing exponentially. Adding to the small space they lived in, the housecat just gave birth to a litter of kittens. My grandparents were adamant that he get rid of all the cats. (I was almost sure this tale was headed down the same dark path. But I let him continue.)

My dad had rounded up the mother and kittens, placed them in a box and tied it to the back of his motorbike. He drove them out of town, up one of the many mountains that make up the Bekaa Valley, and down another road, unloading them about 10 miles from home. But less than two days later, the mama cat showed up on the family patio.

"Amazing story?" my dad asked.

"Yes, Dad," I confirmed, dumbfounded. "Quite amazing, indeed."

As it turns out, occurrences of cats traveling great distances to get where they want to be are not all that uncommon. In 1973, a man named John Sutcliffe gave his ginger kitten to his grand-daughter, who lived 150 miles away. Three weeks later, John found the cat lounging on his front doorstep, waiting for her original owner. John didn't think anything of it, but his wife immediately made the connection and confirmed it with her granddaughter, who admitted that the cat had escaped weeks earlier.

Another pet, named Beau Cat, was temporarily left home while its Louisiana family looked for a new home in Texas. When they returned home, the cat was gone, and they did not see it for five months, at which time it reappeared—in Texas—in a schoolyard where the mother of the family was a teacher and her son, a student.

The ability of animals to travel long distances with the purpose of finding a specific place or thing, and actually finding it, is called "psi trailing." Psi trailing remains a pseudoscience with unsupported evidence, but those rare researchers who do study the phenomena believe there is enough empirical evidence to assume it's very real.

The way psi trailing works is a complete mystery. Several theories attempt to explain the phenomenon with everything from telepathy to magnetic fields in the soil, to Bell's theorem acting from the closeness of animals to their companions (the theory suggests that electrons work in pairs, each one continuously rotating on an opposite axis from its partner, and if one is spun from clockwise to counter clockwise, or vice versa, its partner will adjust and rotate opposite to the new direction).

The term psi trailing was coined by Dr. Joseph Rhine of Duke University, who studied cases of incredible journeys by pets traveling with an emotional and humanlike intent. Dr. Rhine was very professional in his research, remaining a skeptic until the answers were clear-cut and right in front of him. Together, Rhine and his daughter, Sara Feather, sought out and confirmed many cases of psi trailing, at least to their standards. The father and daughter team identified substantial markings on the animal—not just color commonalities, but actual unique markings or anomalies that would be unlikely to appear in the same way, in the same place, on the same colored cat, more than once.

The most famous report of cat psi trailing investigated by Rhine and Feather is that of a Californian cream-colored Persian named Sugar. She was the pet of the Woods family, who lived in Anderson, California. In 1952, Mr. Woods was a retired school principal who wished to move his family to a farm in Gage, Oklahoma. Knowing that Sugar was terrified of car rides, Mr. Woods made the difficult decision to leave her behind with a neighbor.

One year and two months later, a cream-colored Persian jumped onto Mrs. Woods' shoulder while she was working in the barn. The cat looked a lot like Sugar, and it behaved much like Sugar, too. But that was not enough evidence for the Woods. Remembering that Sugar's left hip had a bone deformity, the family examined the cat and found the abnormality. They then went through an old phone book and found their California neighbor's phone number. The neighbor confirmed that 13 months earlier, only three weeks after the Woods left Sugar behind, the cat ran away and was never seen again.

If indeed Sugar was one of a kind, without an identical twin or clone, and it was her that appeared on the farm in Oklahoma, she traveled 1550 miles across the California desert and the Rocky Mountains, just to find the people she loved.

The Cat Came Back...With a Vengeance

When firefighter Christopher Cortes exited his home in Coconut Creek, Florida, he found something very undesirable waiting for him on the hood of his Chevy Silverado. Poo. Not the white kind that falls from the sky. No, the kind Christopher found came from some kind of groundling.

Searching for clues, Christopher immediately ruled out a human vandal because of the size of the poo and the light scratches on the truck's hood. Poo was one thing, but scratching his truck—that's another crime entirely.

Nearby, Christopher found the culprit strutting around with his tail wagging in the air.

The suspect had jet-black hair, stood one foot tall on four legs and weighed approximately 8 to 10 pounds. His age, though undetermined, was no younger than three years. Locals knew him as Mr. Kibbles.

Christopher and his fiancé, Iris, debated what to do. They knew Mr. Kibbles lived with the Leonard family next door. They were wholesome neighbors and had been quite helpful in the past. Chris and Iris didn't want to confront the Leonards, especially at that moment, as the youngest Leonard, Maggie, was celebrating her 11th birthday inside the house. But on the flip side, they were not about to let Mr. Kibbles go unpunished. Oh no, something had to be done, and done quickly, before the party was over.

The couple catnapped Mr. Kibbles. Maybe the extreme retaliation was a response to the lack of gratitude Christopher received as a firefighter when he saved cats from trees; he was sick and tired of their furry faces. The decision he and Iris made would eventually come back to haunt them.

Stuffed into the same truck he had just defiled, Mr. Kibbles was going for a short trip to the park, but there would be no picnic. Located 15 miles from Coconut Creek, Everglades National Park is the largest subtropical region of the United States. It is home to the American bald eagle, American crocodiles and the Florida Everglades panther that, though a cousin of Mr. Kibbles, is definitely not an ally.

Whatever fate awaited Mr. Kibbles in the Everglades, Christopher hoped he'd never see Mr. Kibbles' whiskers again.

Christopher, however, feeling somewhat guilty already, rationalized his decision. Because Mr. Kibbles is a wild animal, he assured Iris, he'd thrive in the wilderness, catching tons of robust rodents to dine on. Surely, we're taking him to a better place...or, at the very least, a more challenging one.

It was true that Mr. Kibbles was a wild animal, but he'd been living a pampered life for three years. Found by the Leonards as a stray, he was taken into their home, vaccinated and neutered. He became a regular member of the family, just like Lulu Leonard, the yapping Westie terrier.

Mr. Kibbles, Lulu and the human Leonards were a close-knit group. When the human Leonards took Lulu for a walk, Mr. Kibbles often accompanied them. Perhaps that is how he built up his stamina and honed his incredible sense of direction.

Thinking it was all over, and believing they'd only have fake concern when their neighbors began their search party, Christopher and Iris went on with their day. When they returned home, however, they were surprised to find Maggie's dad, Peter, waiting for them. Perhaps he'd witnessed their catnapping, or maybe he just had a bad feeling about Christopher. Peter immediately confronted his neighbor with accusations of criminal conduct.

Christopher didn't deny any of it, but he did conjure up some excuses. At first, he claimed that he hadn't known it was their pet, telling Peter that he was just trying to relocate the stray before it was picked up and "put down." Peter wasn't buying it. Christopher changed tactics and repeated his Mr. Kibbles-should-be-so-lucky theory. Peter wasn't hearing that one either.

After much arguing and legal threats, Peter returned to his daughter to give her the sad news. Maggie took the news badly, but her family comforted her with deep prayer that night. Maybe it was the work of a divine creator, maybe it was the work of psi trailing or maybe it was the work of one smart cat, but two weeks later, Mr. Kibbles was back home.

It was just another day at the Leonards' residence, now devoid of meows and purrs. Suddenly, the family heard Lulu barking at something on the other side of the front door, and she just wouldn't stop. When Maggie opened the door to investigate, a familiar feline waltzed right into the house, brushing itself against her leg.

It was a joyous reunion, and the Leonard family was whole again. But Mr. and Mrs. Leonard were not about to let those trickster neighbors get away with their crime. The Leonards pressed charges against the couple: one count of animal cruelty and one count of misdemeanor theft under $5000, though Mr. Kibbles was certainly worth more than that to his owners.

Christopher and Iris were both convicted. Newly married, together Mr. and Mrs. Cortes served 100 hours and 50 hours respectively in community service. Today, Mr. Cortes is still on active duty as a firefighter. There are no recent reports of him having saved any cats stuck in trees.

It's not known whether Mr. Kibbles used telepathy, magnets or Bell's theorem to find his home. It's possible that he just followed a road or two. Or maybe he memorized the way to the Everglades from the truck ride, and he just followed it back. Not all cats use psi trailing to find their way around. As you'll read next, some cats use their wits and imitate humans to get from point A to point B.

Don't Forget Your Bus Paws!

When cats need to get somewhere unknown, they might turn on their psi trailing, like roadsters turn on a GPS device. But when cats know exactly where they want to be, they, like us, can use their feet, or, if they know the right people, get a ride. Take Mr. Pickles, for example.

One day, Ryan Clayton of Bismarck, Arkansas, got a surprising call from Panhandle Animal Welfare Society informing him that they had custody of his cat, Mr. Pickles, three states away in Florida. Mr. Clayton knew that his cat had been missing for several days, but in Florida? *No*, he thought, *that's impossible*.

But Mr. Pickles actually was in Fort Walton Beach, Florida, more than 600 miles away. It turns out that as Mr. Clayton's new Floridian neighbors were moving in, his cat was set to replace them on the gulf. Mr. Pickles curiously hopped aboard the moving van, which was heading back to Florida after the movers had unloaded the furniture. The driver discovered him the next day in the Orange State.

When Mr. Pickles was returned to Bismarck, he arrived with a shirt that read, "My cat went to Fort Walton Beach and all I got was this lousy T-shirt."

❧◆❧

Liz Bullard of Bournemouth, England, has a regular morning routine. After eating breakfast with her husband, teenage son, two dogs and four cats, she and her son get into the family Toyota Land Cruiser and she drops him off at school. Her morning isn't over just yet; she has one more errand to run. Two miles away from home, she pulls over, leans to her right and pops open the passenger door. A brown Norwegian Forest cat named Sergeant Podge then hops into the vehicle. Liz shuts the door and takes Sergeant home to finish the leftovers from her other pets.

No, she's not the cat's nanny, nor is Sergeant Podge a celebrity cat and she his chauffeur. Liz is actually his owner. But of their large family, Sergeant Podge is the only one who lives a secret life.

Every night, at about 6:00 PM, the shaggy cat wakes from his slumber and heads out on the town. Where does he go? Liz doesn't know. What is he looking for? Liz is beat on that question too. All she knows is where he'll be the next morning.

Sergeant Podge's double life began in the summer of 2007, when he vanished without a trace. Liz called her neighbors to ask if they had seen him, and she put in a report at the Royal Society for the Prevention of Cruelty to Animals. Four days later, an elderly woman who lived two miles away called Liz to inform her that a cat matching Sergeant Podge's description was in her yard. Liz hopped in her vehicle and made the first of hundreds of trips.

Although she doesn't mind making the trip (it actually amuses her greatly), there are days when it is a big inconvenience, such as on weekends. Because of Sergeant Podge, Liz never gets to sleep in. And when she and her husband take a vacation, they have to arrange for a driver to bring Sergeant Podge home. It doesn't matter the time of year or weather. Even when it rains, Sergeant Podge is out and about, doing whatever it is that cats do when we're not looking.

Liz believes that Sergeant Podge (whose name was once Poppy, until they learned his actual gender and gave him a more manly name) goes out to find food. A woman used to feed him sardines, but she moved into a nursing home, and Sergeant Podge's bonus meals disappeared. It's likely that when he sneaks out every evening and crosses the local golf course to his secret destination, someone has a bowl of fish waiting for him.

It really is amazing what cats will do for fish. The next tale is about a cat with a similar destination but a different route.

⚜

Imagine you're a bus driver. You drive the same route every morning, making the same rounds on the same loop, and if it's not the bus you drove the day before, it's pretty close. It's been your profession for years, so, by now, all the faces of passengers have just amalgamated into one multi-racial, multi-spatial humanoid. That is until, one day, out of the corner of your eye, you witness a small passenger scurry onto the bus and hide under a seat. There's not much you can do but scratch your head and move on. *Did that really just happen?*

Suppose that a couple of days later, at the same time and the same stop, the tiny passenger hops onto your bus again. This time you get a good look. The passenger is a fluffy white cat with a purple collar. It realizes that you see it, so again it scurries and hides under a seat. Other passengers on the bus are also surprised to see the little kitty, and now a female passenger is trying to pet it, but the cat won't go anywhere near her hand. *Well, at least I'm not hallucinating.*

That was probably the first thought that came to mind for Bill Khunkhun and other drivers for Travel West Midlands in the United Kingdom. Between January and April 2007, a white cat would get on the No. 331 Walsall to Wolverhampton, sit for a 480-yard ride, and then get off at the next stop. It was always the same two stops that the cat got on and off at. Drivers named the cat Macavity after the mysterious mouser in T.S. Eliot's poem "Macavity," from *Old Possum's Book of Practical Cats.*

All that can be said about Macavity is that he is male, has a blue right eye and a green left eye, and wears a purple collar with no identification tag. The mysterious cat's owner has never been discovered. Macavity is, however, well fed. Either he has a generous owner, or there's a fish and chips shop in the area where he gets off the bus. Nobody knows for sure who feeds the cat, but witnesses assume it's the latter.

Bill Khunkhun told the *Daily Mail*, "As soon as I open the doors, he jumps on. He seems to like it. It was quite strange at first, but now it just seems normal."

It wasn't long before Macavity gained the courage to crawl out from underneath the seats and sit on one seat, just like the rest of the bus riders. If there's an empty seat, he takes it. And if there isn't, most human passengers are charmed enough to give theirs up, usually at the front of the bus, near the entry door. "He is the perfect passenger," said Bill. "The only problem is he never pays."

Perhaps the strangest thing about Macavity is that nobody has ever witnessed him on his return trip. How he gets home is a mystery. Assuming he doesn't want to risk crossing the street to take the return trip, Macavity must be burning off some of the calories from the fish and chips shop on his way back home.

A representative of Travel West Midlands said that Macavity hasn't been on the No. 331 since April 2007, but many of their drivers and passengers still spot him lurking around the same stop where he used to get on. Maybe his owner was shocked to learn about the pet's secret escapades in the news and forbade the kitty from getting into automobiles with strangers—not for candy, not for fun and especially not for fish.

I'll Believe It When Cats Fly

One of the most traveled felines in the world is a cat made of cotton. Roy B, a stuffed aviator cat, began as a YMCA after-school program mascot. One of the program counselors used him to promote a career as a pilot to the children, ages 5 to 12. So, dressed in aviator goggles and a hat, and wearing a bomber jacket, Roy B traveled from city to city, from one pilot to another, lounging in the cockpit and getting smothered with hugs by female flight attendants.

On his Southwest Airlines travels, the stuffed kitty traveled for six months within America—from Buffalo to Baltimore, Orlando, New York, Los Angeles, Kansas, Vegas and the list goes on. And amazingly, after spending half the year at 14,000 feet in the air, Roy B was only hurt once: a lacerated seam on his paw was quickly stitched up and repaired.

∽◆∾

Aside from being stuffed and purchased from a toy store, Roy B is an exception when it comes to airborne cats. Most cats that fly great distances do so against their will. Cats such as Emily.

When Emily's plane touched down in Milwaukee, she was enjoying her comfy seat in business class, returning from Paris. After the Continental Airlines flight attendant lifted the cage and brought her down to the arrivals gate, there was a plethora of reporters waiting to see Emily the cat. No, Emily was a not a cat food or cat calendar model; she was just your average, one-year-old house cat—playful, independent and naturally curious.

Emily's journey to the other side of the planet began in September 2005. She wandered into the distribution center of a paper company in her native Appleton, Milwaukee. As she lay snug in a paper bale, the last thing on her mind was a trip to the land of wine and cheese, but when the bale was loaded onto a truck, that's exactly where Emily was headed.

First she traveled to Chicago, boarded a ship and floated across the Atlantic to Belgium. From there, she caught another truck ride to Nancy, France, where she was found by the staff of a laminating company. The surprised workers used her tags to track down the veterinary hospital in Appleton where she was once treated. Emily's vet contacted the McElhiney family. The McElhineys contacted the lamination company, who in turn made arrangements with Continental Airlines to fly the cat home, free of charge, in the lap of luxury.

❧◆❧

Andrea Barlow was in a Munich airport, waiting for her luggage to slide onto the conveyer belt and glide toward her. She had just arrived from England on a United Airlines flight but still had a long way to go before reaching her destination in Washington, DC. When her bags came into view, she packed them onto the dolly and moved on to the fragile arrivals to retrieve her caged cat, Pumpkin, a 12-year-old orange tabby. But as the cage approached, her heart began to race.

At first, it seemed as though her mind was playing a trick on her—*that's not a broken door on the cage that I'm seeing, is it? Wait a second, why is the cage empty?* As the conveyer belt brought the cage closer to her, she hoped that it was someone else's carrier—people mistake others' luggage for their own all the time, maybe there were two of the same carriers on board. It wasn't until she had the carrier in her hand that she knew it was Pumpkin's.

Andrea immediately contacted representatives of United Airlines, who looked for the kitty but to no avail. Her cat was gone, and her flight had to depart. Wherever Pumpkin was, Andrea doubted she'd ever see her again. She continued on with her trip to Washington, feeling sad and desperate, recalling the great times she shared with Pumpkin and coping with the thought that they might not meet again.

But three weeks later, the plane Andrea had been on was undergoing maintenance in Denver, and Pumpkin was found in a pressurized area of the cargo hold. She was emaciated and terrified but alive. One can only guess how many cities and countries she'd been to, or how many sick bags she used up.

When United Airlines contacted Andrea, joy washed over her. Pumpkin was found—alive—and only a few states away. But instead of making her retrieve Pumpkin, the airline flew the cat to her—in coach, and in the lap of a company representative. The rep kept a tight grip on the carrier, making sure there was no repeat of Pumpkin's dash and escape.

❧❖❧

It's a shame that Ozzy, a native of Qatar now living in the United Kingdom, didn't collect Air Miles. If you total up the distance between Qatar and England—6300 miles—and multiply it by the number of days he spent in a plane cargo hold, and how many trips between the two countries the plane made in that time, Ozzy traveled well over 37,000 miles.

As with Pumpkin, Ozzy's owners experienced a dreadful desperation. During a changeover in Dubai, they discovered his carrying case was empty as it slid past them in luggage claims. British Airways did their best to track down Ozzy. They worked with an Abu Dhabi city paper and put up missing kitty posters around the airport.

Ten days later, their efforts paid off and Ozzy was found in Abu Dhabi, still in the same plane he began his travels on. And so he was reunited with his owners in his new home.

❧❖❧

It wasn't until Rob Carter arrived at his Fort Worth, Texas, hotel that he realized he might have grabbed the wrong suitcase at the airport. As his luggage lay on the bed, he cracked it open and immediately realized it was someone else's. He probably sighed to himself, maybe even smacked himself on the forehead, and then reached to close it so that he could head back to the airport while there was still time to exchange it.

But just as he was about to close the suitcase, a kitten leaped from the bag and hopped onto the blanket, then to the floor and under the bed. Rob Carter told the *Associated Press*, "I screamed like a little girl."

He tried to coax the kitten, named Gracie Mae, out from under the bed, but it wouldn't budge. It spent the entire night there, hiding against the wall with its eyes wide open. In the morning, Rob managed to coax the kitten toward him. He got a good look at her tag and called the number on it.

Meanwhile, in Palm Beach Gardens, Florida, 24-year-old Kelly Levy was exhausted from pulling out her bathroom tile floors and the removing the cabinet, all to find her missing cat, which she thought might be hiding in the crawl space. No such luck. The last time she saw Gracie Mae was when her husband was packing his luggage for a trip to Texas. When Kelly returned home from driving him to the airport, she didn't see Gracie Mae sitting on the bottom step, as she usually did when Kelly walked through the front door.

Panicked, she turned the house upside-down looking for the kitten and covering the neighborhood with posters of Gracie Mae's portrait. She called her dad to help her remove the bathroom fixtures so that they could peek into the crawl space. And after all that effort, Gracie Mae was still missing. Suddenly, Kelly's phone rang. When Kelly answered it, the caller gave her no time to speak: "Hi, you're not going to believe this, but I am calling from Fort Worth, Texas, and I accidentally picked up your husband's luggage. And when I opened the luggage, a cat jumped out," said Rob, according to Kelly's media interview.

So how Gracie Mae ended up in Texas was obvious, but now Rob and Kelly wanted to know how she survived the journey, and more incredibly, how nobody noticed her or heard her cries until Rob found her. Gracie Mae's ordeal involved being stuffed in a suitcase that was strapped closed, being packed into a car, driven across the city, carried to baggage handlers, put on a baggage belt and through an x-ray machine, loaded onto a plane with the caution you'd give any non-fragile luggage, and flown 1500 miles at 14,000 feet.

Although Rob was happy to help an animal-loving stranger, he admits that he was slightly disappointed. Had he not found Gracie Mae's owner, he planned on keeping the cat and naming her "Suitcase."

The Queen/King of Antarctica

Harry McNeish was 64 years old when he died in September 1930. Accounts of his last days are depressing. He was sick and frail, and constantly dwelling on one moment from his life. As he aged and withered, it was not uncommon to hear McNeish mutter the same thing over and over again. With lethargic rage, he would repeat under his breath, "Shackleton shot my cat."

A Glasgow native, McNeish was the onboard carpenter of the prestigious ship *Endurance* in 1912. Fellow crewmembers called him "Chippy," a colloquial British term for "carpenter." Before he left Glasgow for the expedition, Chippy found a tiger-striped tabby lounging in his toolbox. Enamored by the cat, he took it with him on the ship. The crew, jocularly marrying the cat to McNeish, named it Mrs. Chippy. But Mrs. Chippy was not a she. One month after docking, the crew discovered Mrs. Chippy was actually a Mr., and, because the crew was unwilling to have two Mr. Chippys on board, the name stuck. Gender didn't matter to them anyway. What did matter was personality, and Mrs. Chippy had plenty of it.

A proficient mouser, Mrs. Chippy impressed the ship's crew with his stellar hunting abilities. Mrs. Chippy could eradicate rodents so swiftly that even the ship's leader, the legendary Sir Ernest Shackleton, found him amazing. The cat became one of the crew.

At first, Mrs. Chippy was known to follow Mr. Chippy like a needy wife, but soon he broke out and made more friends. His new friends fed him only the very best foods, and he was treated much more valuably than the 70 Canadian huskies kenneled in the lower section of the ship. Day and night, the dogs barked incessantly, and that made Mrs. Chippy stark raving mad. Fed up, he wanted to give those dogs something to bark about. He frequently walked over to the kennels, tormenting the canines with his paw and infuriating them even more with his meowing and hissing. The dogs would swipe back at him, but incredibly, they never managed to get a good shot at the cat.

He also displayed excellent balance. The crew was awed by his ability to tread the ship's rails, even when the sea was extremely tumultuous. Most of the time, he showed off with no consequences, but one night he was unlucky. From the cabin porthole, Mrs. Chippy jumped into the South Atlantic's jet-black, freezing waters. Maybe Mrs. Chippy wasn't cautious, maybe he wanted to swim or maybe, just maybe, he had an ominous feeling—a premonition of the boat's fate as it sailed southbound for Antarctica—and he wanted to get out fast. Whichever it was, he definitely regretted it afterward.

Lieutenant Hubert Hudson heard the kitty's cries, and when he investigated the dock, Mrs. Chippy couldn't be found. He listened more diligently and realized the pleas weren't coming from anywhere on the *Endurance*. Hudson turned the boat around and saved the cat from inevitably turning into a furry Popsicle.

From Glasgow to London, Buenos Aires to Georgia, Mrs. Chippy was a true voyager. He saw more land and ocean in his short life than most people do in a lifetime. But it was in the Antarctic that his journey ended tragically.

Well, actually, tragedy first struck everyone but Mrs. Chippy.

On January 18, 1915, the *Endurance* found herself strangled on all sides by icy Antarctic waters. Completely immobile, she was like an unknown island. The men and animals on the ship patiently waited it out. Mrs. Chippy had no qualms about the cold environment, but he grew more restless and bored than everyone else. He disappeared on February 5 for five days. The crew searched frantically for their shipmate, but it was McNeish who

Cat-toid

A cat in Buenos Aires, Argentina, named Mincho, once climbed up a tree and lived there until she died—six years later! That didn't stop male cats from chasing tail. Mincho had three litters of kittens while in that tree.

was most sorrowful, and, later, most delighted when Mrs. Chippy returned on his own, unharmed.

The crew celebrated his return by giving Mrs. Chippy plenty of delicious seal meat; so much meat that while the rest of the explorers became emaciated and shed weight at an alarming rate, he was getting huskier. Perhaps this made one of the crewmen jealous.

John Vincent, *Endurance*'s boatswain, was irate with Mrs. Chippy and accused him of enraging the dogs. By the scruff of the neck, Vincent held Mrs. Chippy threateningly to the dogs as though offering him up for their dinner. The youngest crewman, Pierce Blackborrow, Mrs. Chippy's second favorite companion, saved the cat and scolded Vincent. He made a formal complaint against the boatswain, who was eventually demoted.

The shipmen found Mrs. Chippy's carelessness courageous. In October 1915, as the men were at the peak of desperation, a crewman wrote the following in his log: "Mrs Chippy's almost total disregard for the diabolical forces at work on the ship was more than remarkable—it was inspirational. Such perfect courage is, alas, not to be found in our modern age." Less than two weeks after the log entry, Sir Ernest Shackleton ordered Mrs. Chippy shot.

It was not meant to be a nefarious gesture. Shackleton had just made the most crucial decision

HARRY McNEISH
DIED 24. SEPT. 1930.

A MEMBER OF THE
IMPERIAL TRANS-ANTARCTIC EXPEDITION 1914-17.
HE ACCOMPANIED SHACKLETON
ON HIS EPIC BOAT JOURNEY FROM
ELEPHANT ISLAND TO SOUTH GEORGIA.

ERECTED BY N. Z. ANTARCTIC SOCIETY.

A life-size sculpture of Mrs. Chippy sits upon the gravestone of dear friend Harry McNeish.

of his life: to abandon the ship. His plan was to sail to Elephant Island on one of three lifeboats built by McNeish. Everything that was deemed unnecessary had to be discarded. Mrs. Chippy was deemed unnecessary.

After it was announced that Mrs. Chippy was on death row, the cat was made king for a day. He was fed a big bowl of sardines, petted and stroked by all that adored him and taken to a tent to sleep. Blackborrow, who wished he could save the cat's life a second time, entered the tent to share a last moment with Mrs. Chippy.

McNeish, however, had little time to spend with his feline friend because he had too much work to do on the lifeboats. Unable to say good-bye in a meaningful way—and because he had to say goodbye at all—McNeish became angry with Shackleton.

Already on Shackleton's bad side, McNeish's resentment of the leader never waned. Even as they sailed together in the same lifeboat, their relationship only worsened. The biggest blow came after the entire rescue mission was over and the men of *Endurance* were at last released from the ice's grip. All but four of the crewmen were awarded the Polar Medal. Despite being the carpenter who built the lifeboats that saved all 28 men, McNeish was one of the snubbed four.

Forgiveness was not an option. McNeish took his resentment over the absence of a medal and the death of Mrs. Chippy to his grave. In 2004, 74 years after his death, the New Zealand Antarctic Society hired sculptor Chris Elliot to adorn Harry McNeish's headstone with a life-size sculpture of Mrs. Chippy. In a way, the gravesite pays tribute to two lives: a hardworking seaman and a tenacious cat.

CHAPTER SIX

Catty Criminals

On the Inside

ANIMALS IN CORRECTIONAL facilities are not rare, and they are not new. An 18th-century British asylum successfully rehabilitated inmates by having them work with farm animals. Today, centuries later, pet therapy programs across the world help rehabilitate prisoners so that they ultimately become better citizens.

Several Canadian correctional facilities provide pet therapy, including Nova Institution for Women in Nova Scotia, and Stony Mountain Institution in Manitoba. Edmonton Institution for Women used to have such a program, but too many inmates complained of cat allergies, and the pets were removed. Saskatchewan's Okimaw Ohci Healing Lodge doesn't have an official program, but two cats do live there. Staff and inmates both look after the Okimaw cats.

Studies of inmates partaking in pet therapy programs show that animal companionship behind bars has many positive effects, such as improving a prisoner's self-esteem. Many inmates feel guilt-ridden and lose their sense of humanity while in

This stray cat might find herself in prison, but the only crime she committed was that of compassion.

꒷ꡋ꒦

jail. When given the opportunity to care for an animal, they regain some of their pride.

Inmates learn, or relearn, how to be responsible persons when caring for animals. Programs often have participants groom and train the animals, and look after them like small family members. If the program is successful and the inmate is released, he or she can apply much of the acquired patience and compassion to loved ones at home. If the prisoners never get to see the outside world again, the animals help relieve their loneliness behind bars by giving them something to communicate with or something positive to talk about.

Animals provide a much needed diversion in jail. The harsh surroundings, often more dangerous than the shady streets some of the inmates had prowled, are not a very positive atmosphere. Inmates have to constantly watch their backs, and they worry about their safety among fellow prisoners. But having an animal to care for can relieve some of the stress of their environment. Also, having small animals around the facilities improves the atmosphere; the pets' innocence helps to create a positive environment that reduces stress and violence.

Besides dogs, cats are the most commonly used animals in pet therapy programs. Although cats tend to be associated with women more than with men, one study of a state penitentiary in Switzerland found positive results in the attitudes of the all-male inmates who were allowed to keep cats in their cell block. While interviewing past and present participants in a 1980s experiment called the Cat Programme, researcher Nadine Nef found that most of the men took solace in having a living creature around them that was non-judgmental.

Subjects who cared for cats and were still behind bars expressed happiness in having an acceptable way to give affection in the hostile environment. The cats improved their emotional state in ways comparable to psychiatric help. Some of the jailed individuals admitted that without their cat's companionship, they'd have nothing left to live for. And even the subjects who didn't keep cats enjoyed the program. Simply having the cats around in the TV room or library had a positive effect on the inmates.

Whether it is the companionship, the responsibilities that come with caring for cats or the sense of ownership, cats have made a difference. The Swiss case is especially unique because the program allowed prisoners to actually keep the cats as pets. The cats stayed with them in their cells, and when the inmate was paroled, or his sentence was complete, he had the option of taking the cat home. Many participants did just that.

Where do these jail cats come from? Most of them are rescued from cat shelters, where they were likely to be euthanized. Call it a last act of redemption. Prisoners, some of whom have taken lives, are now saving them. And in return, some of the cats save lives, too.

In a *Globe and Mail* interview, cat behaviorist Diana Partridge described some of the effects cats had on inmates at Indiana State Prison, a maximum-security penitentiary where a majority of the inmates are imprisoned for murder. But before pet therapy was implemented, the prison directors first had to be inspired.

It all began with one homeless cat that lived around the prison grounds and had a litter. The kittens, prohibited in the cells, became a hit on the prison black market, selling for $1000 each.

One of the Indiana inmates told Partridge that he smuggled in a kitten because he feared other inmates would sadistically harm the critter, whom he later named Jinx. The inmate stated that one day he confronted another inmate and was ready to injure or kill him. He told Partridge that after holding onto little Jinx, his aggression receded and he lost his deadly urges, at least for the time being. Stories such as these ultimately led to the prison's official pet-facilitated program.

Like Jinx and his extended family, many cats find their way onto prison grounds by accident and stay for convenience. Prison workers on New York's notorious Rikers Island were aware cats were on the premises but didn't know the exact number. The cats were discovered when an escaped inmate took refuge under a trailer. When guards investigated the trailer, the cats, well over 200 of them, ran out from under it. After the discovery, the New York City Department of

Cat-toid

In Florida, the U.S. Fish and Wildlife Service reports that feral cats are partly responsible for many decreasing wildlife populations, some of which are endangered species. Because the feral cats (about 15 million in Florida) are not a natural part of the state's ecosystem, the food chain has become destabilized.

Corrections teamed up with cat shelters and humane societies to develop a Capture-Neuter-Return (CNR) program. Each time a cat was caught, it was spayed or neutered by one of several generous organizations. The cat was then returned to Rikers to help in keeping another animal population down—the rodents. Other cats were adopted out.

Not all prison cats get there uninvited. At a Mississippi women's prison, homeless and needy cats were delivered to the facility, sort of like it was a feline refugee camp. After Hurricane Katrina crashed into the Gulf Coast in 2005, some 50,000 pets were abandoned, either because their owners were desperate and needed to flee or they had died in the storm. Shelters were overwhelmed with the numbers of animals desperately in need of help, so they resorted to turning some prisons into sanctuaries instead. Pocahontas Correctional Unit in Mississippi had five cats pre-Katrina. Post-Katrina, it was a refugee camp for 25 displaced cats. The inmates, all women, took an instant liking to the kitties and rehabilitated the cats from the trauma they suffered during the hurricane. When it was time to find a home for the orphans, the inmates were reluctant to give them up.

Cat Burglers and Muggers

Don't be fooled by all these studies and stories of inspiration. Not all cats are cute and fluffy. Not all of them save lives or act heroically. Some of them are bad apples—delinquents who deserve to be behind bars.

I got the idea for this chapter while probing newspaper archives. I discovered an article in an October 2007 edition of *Mohave Daily News,* a publication out of Bullhead, Arizona, that reported a violent cat on the loose. Animal Control officers were called in when a woman attempted to pet a cat that she claims "looked friendly," and the cat chomped on her hand. Another incident on the same day involved the same cat. Both victims sought medical treatment immediately. Officers tried to lure the hissing hooligan into a cage, but the cage door broke and the cat escaped.

"The cat is described as a gray and white domestic short hair male, approximately two years old, wearing no collar," wrote the reporter.

A phone number was posted at the end of the article for anyone with information about the fugitive's whereabouts. I called the paper the day after the article was printed. They had found her. When asked what they did about the cat, the person answered, quite ominously, "We took care of it."

∽❖∾

Cat-toid

Every year in the United States, between four and six million cats are euthanized.

Cats steal from us all the time. How many times have you "misplaced" something, only to find it behind the litter box, or somewhere else that's more cat-friendly, like behind the fridge? Let them out of the house, and they might just steal from your neighbors too.

In 2006, Willy the cat angered some citizens of Pelham, New York, because every time they went out to pick vegetables from their garden, their gardening gloves would be missing. The delinquent glove lover had an insatiable affinity for items that looked like hands made of cloth and rubber. No matter what the color or material, Willy wanted the gloves, and he would sneak through every backyard in the suburb to get to them. When he finally got his paws on the neighbor's gloves, he dropped them in his own backyard and forgot about them. His thievery got so out of hand that his owners started hanging up the stolen gloves on a clothesline, and they erected a sign above them reading, "Our cat is a glove snatcher. Please take these if yours."

❧◆❧

Another thief is Elijah from Oxford, Michigan. His story was reported in a January 2001 issue of *Your Cat*. Elijah bullied neighborhood children and stole their teddy bears. He had apparently collected a treasure trove of toys, including dolls, slippers and stuffed rabbits. When his stash was discovered, neighbors gathered to reclaim their possessions as the guilty cat stood by and watched.

❦

And it's not just assault and robbery that cats commit either. Instances of cat arson are more common than one would like to imagine. Take, for example, Felix from Derbyshire, England. Felix was a sickly cat who threw up on his owner's TV. The vomit seeped into the vents of the TV, struck a fuse and caused a fire that destroyed the living room. His owner had no home insurance, and though she and Felix escaped safely, they were almost left homeless.

None of these punk pussycats had to face time, but as you will read in the next story, little Lewie is different. Not only was he punished for his crimes, but his owner was too.

Crime and Punishment

If you haven't been the victim of a dog attack, you probably know someone who has. When I was three years old, twin rottweilers attacked me. My older sister came to my defense and saved me from becoming a chew toy. I've always explained this as being the main reason that I am a cat man. But there is a cat that could turn that all around.

Five-year-old Lewis, a black and white, six-toed (polydactyl) longhair, looks like a big fluffy kitty. But behind those big oval eyes lives the soul of a thug. Lewis, whom the media nicknamed

"The Terrorist of Sunset Circle," attacked at least six people. Although not quite Osama bin Laden, the feline felon did have neighbors and passersby living in fear.

In a Fairfield, Connecticut, neighborhood in 2006, Lewis, or Lewie as his owner called him, earned a reputation for his violent animosity. "His MO is to spring from behind you, and what he does is wrap himself around your legs, and he bites and scratches," neighbor Janet Kettman told the *Associated Press*. "You never see it coming. He has six toes on every foot, which constitutes a very formidable weapon."

Seventy-six-year-old Janet was attacked twice. Like Lewie's other victims, Janet reached a point where she could only leave the house in defense mode, constantly watching her back. She was not Lewie's first victim, but she was the first to take action. After running some errands one evening, she arrived home, got out of her car and made her way to the front door. Suddenly, from under her porch, Lewie emerged and pounced, attacking the back of her right leg. "I never saw it coming," Janet said. By the time the ordeal was over and she shook off the attacker, she was left with three visible bites and eight gouges. That's when she took action and reported the incident to Animal Control.

Lewie was apprehended, and Janet identified him in a cat lineup, which resulted in the first restraining order against him. The order said that he could only be outside for half a day, mostly past the neighbors' bedtimes. He was force-fed calming medication—Prozac for cats. From December to February, Lewie was a good boy...or at least a law-abiding one. But after two months under house arrest, Lewie was back to his criminal ways.

His owner, Ruth Cisero, was feeling under the weather. She rested in bed knowing that as long as Lewie was inside the house somewhere, then he was not a worry. Her boyfriend arrived to bring her pizza and spend time with her. Sometime between the boyfriend's arrival and his entry into the home, Lewie made a swift escape. It was as if he was eager for just one more crime; he acted quickly and attacked another neighbor.

It was the last straw. Lewie was facing hard time.

Lewie's life was called into question. It looked as though Lewie was to get the harshest punishment—the death penalty. But after a plea bargain with Ruth's attorney, Judge Patrick Carroll gave Lewie and Ruth softer sentences. He ordered the defendants to keep Lewie inside the house at all times, the only exceptions being visits to the vet. No outdoor play. No walks. No travel. The judge gave them one last chance, and if Lewie left the house again, even accidentally, he would be put in the hands of Animal Control and most likely put down. The incentive for Ruth was equally serious. Another escape by Lewie could result in her serving up to six months in prison on charges of second-degree reckless endangerment.

So, with Lewie under permanent house arrest, and Ruth serving two years probation, a support group emerged. On the popular social networking website, My Space, a devoted Lewis lover set up a profile in support of the feline. Over 500 "Save Lewis" T-shirts were sold to raise money for Ruth's defense fund, and animal rights protesters wore the shirts to her and Lewie's trial. Best Friends, an animal sanctuary in Utah, offered to take Lewie in if he were sentenced to death. Ruth graciously declined. Lewie is a devoted pet, and she is a devoted pet owner. He belongs with her no matter the curfew or conditions.

Since the time Ruth adopted Lewie, a stray that showed up at her door, Ruth, Lewie and her two other cats have been a tight-knit family. She believes that Lewie gets angry and attacks only because he's been provoked. She claims that most of the complaints come from other cat owners, and it's their cat's fault for bringing out the worst in Lewie. She recalls one occasion in which Lewie was water hosed by a neighbor. Everyone knows cats hate water. Perhaps this was enough to send him over the edge.

To date, still on Prozac and still living with Ruth and her other cats, Lewie has managed to keep himself out of the news and inside the house.

If It Doesn't Hiss, You Must Acquit

It took the jury only two hours to dismiss the charges against the black and white, whiskered defendant as frivolous. But by the time the four-year-long case finally ended, LC, or "Library Cat," was long dead.

It all began one November afternoon in 2000. Rik Espinosa, a journalist for the community paper, entered the Escondido Public Library in San Diego with his dog to research an article. Rik saw a sign that stated "No Animals," but he knew it didn't apply to Kimba because she was his assistance dog. He didn't expect that another animal would be there, too—one that made her home in the library. LC has been a resident library cat in the small town since 1994.

On that particular November day, LC awoke from a snooze she was having on a shelf. Her eyes still shut, she yawned, arched her back and stretched. She opened her eyes and reacted to what she saw near her: a predator. She hopped off the shelf onto the floor and took a pre-emptive strike against the dog.

Cat-toid

According to the *Guinness World Records* book, a ginger tabby named Jake has the most toes of any feline. Each of Jake's paws has seven digits.

According to Rik, LC swatted the dog with "all four paws" and clawed her face, drawing blood. Because of his cat allergies, Rik wasn't about to halt the scuffle hands-on. Instead, he tried to protect Kimba by dragging the 55-pound Labrador to safety. In doing so, he hurt his back and had a panic attack, something not so rare for Rik—his condition was the reason he had Kimba; he claims that the dog can sense his panic attacks before they occur and put him at ease.

Aside from his back problems and panic disorder, Rik's disabilities were extensive: chronic pain syndrome, major depressive disorder, borderline personality disorder and decreased lung function. In addition, the incident with LC caused him, according to his defense, "significant lasting, extreme and severe mental anguish and emotional distress including, but not limited to, terror, humiliation, shame, embarrassment, mortification, chagrin, depression, panic, anxiety, flashbacks, nightmares, loss of sleep..." The list really does go on. He also said that he suffered additional embarrassment from people ridiculing him and his "wuss dog."

The total cost of medical and vet bills and lost wages resulting from the incident was $325. His requested compensation was $1.5 million. It's no wonder that Rik, once a news writer, was now a newsmaker.

Rik didn't see this as an ordinary dog and cat scrap; this was a violation of his civil rights. According to *The North County Times*, where he was once employed, he believed the city was denying him access to the library by simply having the cat there. He said they put the welfare of LC above his own and that of others with disabilities.

The city's attorney, Steve Nelson, saw things a tad differently—this wasn't a case of discrimination; it was a case of property damage. And the property in question was Kimba, which the city twice offered to "repair," in addition to offering two settlements, one of $1000 and another of $1500. Rik rejected both.

Early on, it seemed that the jury would not be persuaded by Rik's claims. Although only a few pieces of evidence were needed, Rik had 29 exhibits, including a picture of himself with Muhammad Ali, because he believed it gave him credibility.

LC, on the other hand, was getting major sympathetic publicity. Supporters sent emails to her and the library, and fans started dropping by the library to meet the famed feline. But her credibility was shaken a few months after the incident when she attacked another dog. After this second attack, witnesses of a past incident that occurred two years before the one with Kimba came forward with claims of a third attack, involving a dog named Toto and his 11-year-old owner, who was brought to tears.

Without a picture of LC and Muhammad Ali, who would believe in LC? To err on the side of caution, the city evicted her and sent her to live with one of the library employees.

LC developed multiple tumors, which triggered a fatal seizure, and she passed away in 2003. She died still accused, her name still tainted.

However, in 2004, four years after LC's alleged hate crime, all three charges filed against the city of Escondido and LC were dropped. But for LC, it was one year too late.

Jadwiga vs. Goliath

Oregonian Jadwiga Drozdek had a lot of cats, six to be exact. So naturally, she had a lot of cat food stocked up. She also kept a stash of cat snacks in her garage. Over the course of four months, she noticed the food vanishing rapidly, and yet her six pets were as trim as ever. Surely they weren't bingeing and purging. These weren't super model cats; they were regular house cats. And besides, if that were the case, she would be literally stepping all over the evidence.

One January day in 2007, Jadwiga heard a huge hubbub coming from her garage. She entered the garage expecting raccoons. When she saw what she saw, she burst out laughing. She found the big, fat answer to her big, fat mystery—a big, fat cat was stuck in the garage door cat flap.

Jadwiga freed him from her garage door and served him a plate of food on the patio to show him that there was an easier way to get to the stash without stealing. Jadwiga loved animals so much that the big cat need only paw at her door to get what he wanted. But sensing that this cat was more high maintenance and needy than the average cat, she did not take him in.

Assuming he was someone else's bundle of joy, she took him to the Oregon Humane Society (OHS). "Goliath" was the name OHS gave the whiskered mammoth, who was described as having a head the size of a basketball. His girth was so wide that most people struggled to pick him up with two hands. After taking custody of Goliath, OHS started searching for his owner. Charmed by the fat cat, Oregon media covered the story and word spread nationally. Of course, whenever a cute face without a home shows up on TV, there's a mob of people just begging to make it a part of their family. Only Goliath wasn't up for grabs so soon.

Goliath had to have an owner. How else could he bubble up to such an enormous size? No stray has access to that much food. The owner had three days to claim him; otherwise, he'd be put up for adoption.

The mass attention paid off. The very next day, his long-time owner spotted Goliath on TV. Amazingly, they hadn't seen each other for over six months. In many ways, Goliath was a stray. He had been one for at least half the year, wandering Oregon and feeding on anything that resembled food. Goliath, whose real name was Hercules, was reunited with his beloved companion Geoff Earnest, and the reunion was sweeter than anyone could have predicted.

Some time before Hercules disappeared, Geoff was diagnosed with cystic fibrosis. He had to leave Portland for Seattle to undergo a lung transplant. His recovery would take two months, so Geoff made sure Hercules was well cared for with a house sitter.

During Geoff's stay at the University of Washington Hospital, his parents were Hercules' caregivers. Every time they came from Oregon to see him, Hercules was the first thing Geoff asked them about. Strangely, they glossed over the subject, changed the topic or just ignored his questions completely. Something was amiss.

After fully recovering, Geoff learned that Hercules was gone. He couldn't blame his parents for withholding the information. Pictures of Hercules were propped up in his hospital room. The cat was Geoff's best bud, and the last thing his parents wanted Geoff to worry about in his fragile state was that he would never see Hercules again. The cat was presumed "put down."

After two months of suspicions and denial, with an additional four months of grief and acceptance, Geoff's emotions were thrown into the air again when he saw big Herc alive inside the electronic box in front of him. He immediately packed some pictures and videos he had of Hercules to properly claim him from the OHS.

Hercules was back in his life, and just in time to try out the new cathouse Geoff had been building just in case the improbable happened.

Hercules' notoriety attracted some pretty strange characters. A Canadian woman contacted Geoff seeking some of Hercules' sperm or offspring. Unfortunately for her, and Geoff, who could have profited, Hercules was neutered long ago.

While Hercules was enjoying his stay at OHS, some sad news was learned. During his stray days, he had acquired Feline Immunodeficiency Virus (or FIV, the feline version of HIV). But as long as Hercules is kept inside to prevent him from spreading the illness or catching something that threatens his immune system, he can live a full, healthy life. OHS workers say he's actually quite healthy, despite his humongous size. But, of course, he could lose a few pounds.

Despite his criminal past, Hercules has garnered interest from Purina, which has offered to put Hercules on their diet cat food and maybe use him to endorse their product. It goes to show that with a little "purrsonality," you can pretty much wiggle your way out of anything.

The Klepto Kitty

Ruby Montgomery couldn't explain what was lurking about her home in Vancouver, British Columbia. In 1988, whenever she came home from work, she was puzzled to find a light on, the answering machine turned off, the phone unhooked and her jewelry missing. *Surely this place hasn't been invaded by poltergeists,* she thought. Before she had to usher in a ghostbuster or conduct any séances, Ruby found her mischievous spirit.

Ruby was asleep in bed one evening when, suddenly, the lights flashed on. She froze, her eyes focused on the light switch. There was her cat, Suki, standing on her two back paws atop the trunk by the door, splayed against the wall with her claws on the light switch. Suki was caught red-pawed. Ruby raised her brow at the cat, and Suki, sensing she was in deep doo-doo, flicked off the switch and ran out of the room.

Ruby said after that incident, her entire home was covered in masking tape. "Whatever could be picked up or turned off, I had to cover with tape."

Ruby Montgomery is a boisterous and exuberant actress. She is a natural joker, always playful and always taking cracks at her peers. It seems her

Siamese took on many of her traits. Actually, Suki seemed to be on a path to eccentricity from the moment of her planned conception.

Ruby's sister, like Ruby, was a lover of cats. She took the relationship with her feline so seriously that after learning she was pregnant, her biggest fear was that a new baby would make her cat jealous. Ruby's sister decided that to occupy her cat while she attended the new baby, she would get her cat knocked up two months before the baby was due. The plan worked. The two females gave birth one week apart. While Ruby's sister was busy trying to feed her new son, her cat was trying to manage five kittens.

Suki is one of those five offspring, so her cunning was written in the stars. She was always mischievous. Aside from her fixation with turning electronics on and off, she was a kleptomaniac. Suki was such a stellar thief that Ruby had to fool her into hiding the booty in a place where she could always find it, a toy box. "Anything that rolled, she'd take it," claims Ruby. Her lipsticks and earrings were a personal favorite of Suki's. "She'd steal one earring, try it out, and if she liked it, come back for the pair."

According to Ruby, Suki also had a tendency to steal anything red. When Ruby stitched fabrics at her sewing machine, Suki would snatch a spool of red thread and run with it, until the thread unfurled and Suki was left with just the spool (which in itself was a great score because it rolled so splendidly).

Nothing of Ruby's was considered sacred. Not even her purse. "She always went through my purse when I got home and would find the toy or treat I had for her. Seemed cute at first, until I found out she was going through everyone's purse. I was always returning things to guests from her toy box."

Because Ruby carried Suki everywhere—including friends' homes—Suki spent a lot of time in a cat carrier. Ruby's friends adored Suki but had a problem with her constant stealing. If Suki found something she liked, she'd take it and hide it under the carrier's carpet.

"Before I could leave anyone's house, I'd always have to check the rug in her cage," Ruby said. One day, Suki and Ruby were over at Ted's house. Ted was Ruby's best friend, and he loved to test Suki. Knowing that Suki loved all things shiny, he hid a diamond ring, only to watch her prance into the room carrying it in her mouth and over to her carrier.

"No, no," said Ruby to Suki, "don't do that." The diamond ring was snatched from Suki and put in a new hiding spot to see if she'd find it. She did. Only this time, as Suki snuck the ring to her stash spot, she kept her face toward the wall, keeping the stolen property from view. Absolutely amazed, Ruby and Ted let her continue.

They watched as Suki lifted the carrier's carpet with one paw and tucked the ring underneath it with the other. Ted took it back, provoking Suki to hate him more than she already did.

Suki absolutely despised Ted, and Ted loved to provoke her. Ever since she was a kitten, Ted would torment her by holding her up to the ceiling fan and let her squirm in his grip. He introduced Suki to her "cousin Doberman," so she could hiss and run, for Ted's own amusement. Because of the early trauma he inflicted upon her, Suki gave Ted the cold shoulder and stink eye for all 17 years of her life.

"She just couldn't be around him," Ruby said. "She hated everything about him, the sound of his voice, everything. If I came home and checked my messages, and the volume was off, I'd know Ted called." If Suki heard Ted's voice on the machine, she'd use her paw to slide the volume bar to zero, something she learned to do when she was a kitten—Ruby would call from work to leave her a message so that Suki could hear her voice.

But that was only on the days when Suki was home alone. As mentioned, Ruby usually took Suki everywhere she could, and as smart as Suki was, she never grasped the difference between a good or a bad time to come along for the journey. "Once, I was driving to work. I looked next to me, and I saw her poking her little head out of my work bag. I'm like, 'Here we go again,' as I u-turned home."

Although the cat was conniving, mischievous and dominating, Ruby absolutely adored Suki. And despite her evils, Suki was the greatest alarm clock. The clever cat learned to read 12:00 on a clock and woke Ruby up every day at noon for work. Amazingly, Suki, who did not know when she should or should not accompany Ruby on an outing, could tell the difference between a work-day and a day off. "I have no idea how she figured that out," said Ruby. "She just knew when to wake me up and when not to."

Meet the Hemingways

If you log onto the website for the Ernest Hemingway Home & Museum in Key West, Florida, you can watch a live video feed of the yard. It's black and white, grainy and about as thrilling as watching grass grow, but every couple of minutes, a small blur streaks across the scene. Those blurs are caused when one of the more than 50 Hemingway cats crosses the lawn.

If you could zoom in and focus on the paws of most of the cats, you'd find a strange abnormal-ity—polydactylism. Some call these cats "mitten cats," because the extra digit gives them the appearance of wearing furry mittens. Others call these cats "Hemingway cats," because of their notoriety as the famous writer's obsession. But there are also others who call these cats criminals, specifically the United States Department of Agriculture (USDA). They're considered criminals not because of their abnormalities, but because they're illegally exhibited at the Hemingway Home & Museum.

Ernest Hemingway is often thought of as a macho man's macho man: a chauvinist with a gun in one hand and a cigar in the other, sitting by a bottle of whiskey. But despite being an avid hunter, Hemingway was an animal lover. His passion for cats had a lot to do with his upbringing. His mother was an ailurophile, and his father regularly rescued and adopted cats and dogs. When Ernest was a child, his cat lost its tail in a slammed door, and Ernest would watch closely as his dad treated the cat.

When Hemingway lived in France as a starving writer, he was too poor to afford a cat. After establishing himself as one of the greatest writers of our time, he purchased a house in Cuba where more than 50 cats roamed freely. In his letters to America, Hemingway often wrote about his cats. One of his cats shared his affinity for alcohol and was fed whiskey and milk. He even tucked away a copy of Doris Bryant's *The Care and Handling of Cats: A Manual for Modern Cat Owners* next to his bed.

To some extent, Hemingway thought he knew what cats wanted, or at least what they wanted when it came to being named. He believed that cats liked the slithering sound of the letter "S," so he gave his cats names such as Spendy, Shopsky, Ecstasy and Snow White. The now famous extra-clawed "criminals" seen in the video are descendants of Snow White.

Snow White, a Maine Coon, was given to Hemingway by ship captain Stanley Dexter in Key West in 1935. (Some reports claim the cat's name was "Snowball," but that is almost certainly wrong.) The kitty had six toes on its front paws and five on the back. The dominant gene was passed down for countless generations. In 1964, three years after Hemingway committed suicide, his Key West mansion was opened as a museum, and since then, the cats have owned the place. They are all well nourished, "fixed," vaccinated and cared for by a vet who attends them on weekly house calls. The deceased ones are buried in a cemetery on the premises.

The cats have prestigious names given to them by the museum operators. A feline Pablo Picasso, Simone de Beauvoir, Sofia Loren, Charlie Chaplin, Ava Gardner, and Mark Twain make up the current residents, and it wasn't long before tourists, mostly from docked cruise ships, were coming to the mansion to meet these four-legged, six-toed artists, actors and philosophers.

"People come in and they don't know who Hemingway was. They ask what year was he the president," Bob Smith, a guide at the museum, told *USA Today*.

And therein lies the problem. The USDA sees it this way: as long as people are willing to pay to view these cats, the cats are an exhibition, and it is illegal to exhibit animals without a license. But this reasoning is actually a pretense. Like Lewis, the feline assailant put under court-ordered house arrest, these polydactyls got in trouble because of neighbors' complaints.

Neighbors say the naughty cats occasionally climb over a six-foot wall, leave the grounds and cause a nuisance on Whitehead Street, where the Hemingway Home is located. Under the USDA Animal Welfare Act, exhibited animals must be caged, as they would be in a zoo, whether or not they're domesticated. Caging the cats is all the neighbors could ask for to get the Hemingways out of their hair. In the investigation, the USDA sent undercover workers to the museum to take photographs and videos to further their case.

But museum chief executive Mark Morawski wasn't easily persuaded. He read through the USDA requirements and complied, not by caging the cats, but by building an angled fence atop the wall. The USDA still wasn't happy, and the Hemingway Home was still denied a license, so Morwaski took the government to court.

The case began in 2003. It cost American tax-payers more than $17,000. USDA reps made

regular visits to the home and even forced the owners to construct an electrical fence on the property,
which was a total disaster and actually harmed the
cats. And what did the USDA get out of it? Well, as
of January 2008, the case still has no end in sight;
however, the proceedings seem to be in favor of
the museum.

The Key West City Commission backed the
Hemingways, exempting the museum from
a city bylaw that limits houses to four domestic
animals, and inevitably initiated a reprieve of
the case. And the cats have plenty of supporters.
A petition to save them and preserve their place
on the property has accumulated thousands of
signatures. It seems that the cats are more
beloved than the government.

Cat-toid

Many legendary writers were very fond of
felines. Mark Twain, Raymond Chandler,
Charles Dickens, Edgar Allen Poe and T.S.
Elliot, who wrote a book of poems about
cats, were dedicated cat owners.

CHAPTER SEVEN

Pussycat "Purrsonalities"

TAKE A WALK DOWN Hollywood Boulevard and keep your eyes on the sidewalk. As you stroll across the Walk of Fame, you'll see the names of actors, actresses, singers and directors, among others. You'll even read some names of cartoon characters and puppets, such as Bugs Bunny and Kermit the Frog. The only salutes to real celebrity animals are, not surprisingly, all dogs—Lassie, Rin-Tin-Tin and Strongheart.

Everybody knows that dogs can be trained to perform, guide the blind or sniff out illegal substances. When it comes to movies, dogs monopolize the silver screen. You can probably name a number of famous TV dogs, but can you name even one famous TV cat?

Some years ago, I was working in the camera department for a Disney movie about talking dogs. On a farm where a large portion of the movie was filmed, there were about 25 dogs, 12 pigs, a wolf and a billy goat, but not a single cat. Not one! They were totally unrepresented.

Occasionally, cats do appear on screen, but they're used more as background props than actual characters. Yes, they're more difficult to train than canines. Felines are independent and usually aloof. They're scavengers who can find food almost anywhere, so a little treat isn't going to cajole them into doing what you want them to do for however long you want it done, and the hot, bright lights and large, noisy crowds smother them.

A Cat with a Campaign

When cats do achieve celebrity status, it's usually as part of a media-covered story, much like some of the stories in this book. Other cats are used as mascots for businesses and gain notoriety for it. Everybody knows Morris the Cat, the chubby and stern orange tabby who has been peddling 9Lives cat food since the 1960s.

The original Morris (since 1975, there have been several Morrises) was saved from Hinsdale Humane Society in Illinois—and I do mean saved! When professional animal trainer Bob Martwick spotted and adopted him, Morris was only 20 minutes from euthanization (hence his original name, Lucky). As the spokescat for 9Lives, Morris literally talked consumers into buying his brand, with a little help from a voice actor, of course. (As I learned on the Disney set, animals can't actually talk.) Every 9Lives product sports Morris' paw signature of approval.

Morris did get a shot at acting, but in only one movie, *Shamus,* starring Burt Reynolds, in 1973. The cat's movie career was short lived, but he (and his understudies) went on to author three books on pet health and pet ownership: *The Morris Approach, The Morris Method* and *The Morris Prescription.* But his most challenging roles came in 1988 and 1992, when he ran for president of the United States of America on the Finicky Party ticket. Apparently, however, his good nutrition platform wasn't enough to sway voters. He was beaten twice, first by George H.W. Bush and then again by Bill Clinton.

Despite Morris' celebrity, he never forgot his roots. As a sign of gratitude to his savior 40 years ago, he embarked on a national campaign to rescue cats from shelters. Morris' Million Cat Rescue is a traveling bus with Morris and his newly adopted buddy, Li'l Mo, driving across America, promoting adoption from shelters and raising awareness for animal sanctuaries. New cat parents agreeing to adopt one right off the bus get a "Welcome Home" kit, and the organization's goal is to have those kits in the hands of a million people. As of January 1, 2008, Morris helped nearly 700,000 cats find loving homes.

The Bookstore Mascot

In the era of big chain bookstores, independent bookstores can find themselves under water when it comes to advertising. But Oregon's Powell's

Books garnered legendary status partly because of the business' mascot, Fup, a cult favorite among book lovers. She was adopted by Powell's store manager in 1988 and named after the title of a Jim Dodge book.

Fup the cat moved into the bookstore the same day the bookstore moved into its new location in the winter of 1990. During her 17-year stay, she left the premises only once, in 1997 for six weeks, while the store was being renovated. Every other day, she could be found lurking around the bookstore, more fascinated with the leafing of pages than the leaves outside. The employees at the bookstore liked her because she was an avid mouser who made sure that not a single rodent got away. Customers liked her because she was cute and agile, climbing ladders onto bookshelves and monitoring their every movement. Petting her was allowed, but like a ticking time bomb, Fup gave each person only about 30 seconds before she'd sink her teeth into their fingers.

Each week, admirers sent her gifts, cards, letters and emails. In return, she gave them a helpful column in Powell's newsletter. As the years passed, she aged well and was no longer the biting climber she used to be. That gave the staff, customers and her fans a chance to get closer. When she passed away in October 2007, people made donations to the Oregon Humane Society in her name. Fup's legacy survives through her newsletter column.

A Page Turner

Although I had to keep my books enclosed in a cupboard to prevent my cat from turning them into confetti, cats and books actually go together better than you'd think. According to Iron Frog Productions, producers of *Puss in Books: Adventures of the Library Cat*, there were 744 library cats registered as of September 2007. While only 22 have worked in Canada, the United States is home to over 600, including 25 library cat statues, four virtual cats, four stuffed big cats and one ghost cat that haunts a reference room.

There are so many cats that librarian Phyllis Lahti of Minnesota founded the Library Cat Society (LCS) in 1987, inspired by her own library's feline, Reggie. Through the LCS, library employees exchange stories and pictures of their bookshelf mascots. A startling number of their stories start off sad, with an abandoned cat in a parking lot or one dumped in a book chute. But the gentle librarians take the cats in and make them a vital part of the enterprise. Some of their stories are told in Lahti's anthology, *Cats, Librarians, and Libraries: Essays for and about the Library Cat Society*.

In an earlier section, under "Catty Criminals," I wrote about LC, the library cat who attacked an assistance dog and ignited a $1.5 million lawsuit against a public library. Thankfully, not all the library cats in this world are that hostile. Some actually work to relieve stress instead of causing it.

❧◆☙

Vicki Myron, director of Spencer Public Library in Iowa, came to work one January morning in 1988, bundled in layers, heavily scarved and shivering from the walk between her car and the library door. Once inside, she looked at the thermometer: −10° F. Needless to say, she was glad to be indoors again.

She and the morning staff proceeded with their regular opening routine—turning on the lights, printing the unreturned book list and checking in the items dropped in the overnight chute. When she approached the chute, however, she heard a pained mewing coming from inside of it. She lifted the lid. As expected, she found a pile of books and periodicals. But as she emptied the drop-off box to investigate the pitiful plea, she also noticed a wagging orange tail. She reached inside to clear the area and found a shivering, frozen-pawed cat with long orange hair and a long orange neck protruding from the pile of reading material.

Vicki and the other staff began their rescue mission. They warmed the cat up and fed him, surprised that after all his hardships, he still managed to purr throughout. As happy as they were to find him, he was clearly even happier.

After gaining the approval of the library's board of trustees and the Spencer city council, the cat became the official library cat. Vicki took on the role of settling the cat in his new position. She had him declawed, vaccinated and neutered. All he needed was a name.

The library held a contest for patrons to name the cat. Staff members weren't expecting many participants because most of the contests they'd held in the past had only a few entries. But this time was different. Of the 10,000 people living in Spencer, almost 400 entries poured in. The winning entry was Dewey Readmore Books, named after the Dewey Decimal System.

According to his biography on the Spencer Public Library's website, Dewey's job duties include sitting by the entrance doors every morning at 9:00 AM and greeting the patrons; amusing the staff and visitors with his cat antics; providing stress relief for staff, panicked students and researchers; acting as official library ambassador at all round-table meetings; climbing inside every box that enters the library to check its contents and comfort level; curling up inside book bags *just because*; gaining free, worldwide publicity for the library; and becoming the "world's most finicky cat by refusing all but the most expensive, delectable foods."

There was one more thing on his résumé: cheering people up. Outside the library, in people's

homes, Dewey provided something to talk
about—a dinner table distraction from the 1980s
Iowa farming crisis.

Although his meals and medical bills were paid
for by generous donations coming from as far
away as New York, Dewey had a very peculiar
appetite. He liked scrambled eggs, tuna sand-
wiches, Arby's, cheeseburgers, boiled ham and
garlic chicken TV dinners—pretty much whatever
members of the staff were having. But as much as
people loved Dewey, they couldn't deny that he
was a brat.

He loved to climb ladders, no matter how high
or how occupied they were. He was attention
greedy, always climbing onto people's papers,
books and laptops to get that much needed stroke
of his fur. Like all cats, he was an avid napper,
only he preferred the most inconvenient places,
such as open briefcases, and he wouldn't leave
until he was forced to. After crying his way into
screening rooms, he would hop onto the table
and sleep next to the projector lens, his cat ears
probably making an unwanted puppet show on
the screen. And of course, as aloof or sleepy as he
would act during the day, he would get playful
just before closing time. Sometimes staff would stay
a little bit late until he was relaxed and satisfied,
but they weren't being paid overtime for it.

In between guilting the staff into play and incessantly irritating them, Dewey took the time to reply to his pen pals from all over the globe.

It may be indicative of the small town he lived in, but Dewey Readmore Books is the most famous character to come out of Spencer. Aside from his listing in the Library of Congress, Dewey has garnered notoriety as the world's most famous library cat. He's been immortalized in various postcards and in publications such as *Cat Fancy*. He's made several television appearances, the most amazing being when a Japanese television crew flew to Spencer to do a feature on him. Dewey modeled for a cat calendar, and he also made a big appearance in the short documentary, *Puss in Books: Adventures of the Library Cat*. He's even been published, albeit with the help of his good friend Vicki. And today, Dewey is posthumously repaying Vicki for all her help over the years, for both her scribing and feeding.

Cat-toid

Dr. Samuel Johnson (1709–84), lexicographer, poet and essayist, famously adored his cat Hodge, who, in the form of a bronze monument outside the historic scholar's home, stands over a model of Dr. Johnson's most profound work, the *Dictionary of the English Language*.

A year and a half after Dewey Readmore Books lost his bout with stomach cancer and hypo-thyroidism (his obituary ran in 250 publications including *USA Today*), Vicki Myron inked a book deal with Grand Central Publishing worth $1.25 million. The book, *Dewey, a Small Town, a Library and the World's Most Beloved Cat*, is the biography of Dewey and Spencer, and how he changed the town forever.

Cats on the Small Screen

The fact is, you're more likely to find a cat in front of the television than inside of it (and if it is inside the TV, you should probably call an electrician quick!). After learning that 30 percent of cats enjoy watching TV, Meow Mix Co., the same company that brought you Meow Mix Café, made plans with Oxygen Network to air a one-off 30-minute special in May 2003, written and produced specifically for cats. "Oxygen has long been accused of being too pro-dog. Now we are giving cats equal time," said Oxygen CEO and president, Geraldine Laybourne.

With her cat Stinky, Annabelle Gurwich hosted Meow TV. The show included "The Squirrel Alert," in which a squirrel ran up and down a tree, tantalizing the four-legged audience. Public service announcements by and for cats to get spayed and neutered also littered the program. There was "The House Cat Shopping Network," and "Cat Critics," in which large wild cats took cracks at movies à la Mystery Science Theater. Human viewers were also given an opportunity to partake in the show by supplying photos of their cool cats and sending out birthday wishes to their feline friends.

Three years later, in 2006, Meow Mix embarked on their most ambitious project thus far. *Meow Mix House* was a show in which 10 rescued cats from across the United States were placed in a home, pinned against each other in competitions and voted off by a panel of cat behaviorists. Move over *Big Brother,* the first feline reality show had arrived.

The 10 "cat-testants" competed over 10 days, and the program aired in 10, 10-minute episodes on Animal Planet. (For viewers who couldn't wait for the next episode, several cameras were fixed throughout the New York house and broadcasted the live feed online, 24 hours a day.) In every episode, a new cat was voted off, and his or her exclusion determined their results in the competitions and overall interaction with the room-mates. Beth Adelman, an animal behaviorist and show consultant, said a major requirement of the cat-testants was that they "must play well with others."

In the first episode, Belle, a cat from Philadelphia, refused to participate in the Climb-o-Thon and was thus voted off. Another cat-testant, Sam from Dallas, was eliminated for his subpar purring in the Purr-Off. But not all cats were excluded because of their sportsmanship; Romeo was shown the door because of his overactive sex drive.

In the end, the Florida feline Cisco triumphed. The five-year-old orange and white 17-pound tabby was the underdog because of his age and weight, but he impressed judges with his skills in the competitions and his egregious behavior with other cats. He was appointed Feline Vice President of Research and Development of Meow Mix, a position not paid with money, but with loads of food.

Regardless of who won or lost, or who got to stay longer and who didn't, all the cats were winners. After each cat left the house, each one moved directly into another home, one with a loving human family, happy to adopt.

Television entertainment aside, every now and then, a cat appears in the foreground of the silver screen. Their presence usually goes unnoticed, but I'd like to take a moment and pay tribute to some of those esteemed cat celebrities.

Working with Legends

In the world of theater, it is common to have a backstage cat around to ease the actors' performance jitters. Theater superstition claims that having a black cat backstage brings good luck, and when any cat wanders on stage, it's even luckier. But what about on a film set?

Does a wandering cat bring good luck? Well, in the case of Pepper, or Pep the Cat, she brought herself good luck with her presence on a film set.

Pep was a gray alley cat that stepped onto a random set in the early 1900s and became a star in the golden silent era of film. She worked with some of the greatest actors of the times, including Charlie Chaplin, Fatty Arbuckle and the Keystone Kops. In her first role in 1917, she played herself, "Pep," in *Are Waitresses Safe?* Her part was small but memorable. In the film, Louise Fazenda, or "Only a Working Girl," as she's credited, works in a restaurant. Everything that can go wrong in the kitchen does. Pep's job was to eat the cuckoo bird from the cuckoo clock. Stellar performance!

Between 1918 and 1928, she performed in 14 movies, usually as an irritating catalyst of trouble. She often shared the screen with her gigantic but tender friend Teddy, a Great Dane. The two were inseparable. Sadly, shortly after her co-star died, Pep left the industry, too. She simply disappeared and was never seen again.

⋘◆⋙

Moving from the silent movies to the talkies, this is the story of Orangey, Audrey Hepburn's memorable co-star in *Breakfast at Tiffany's.* Orangey, a longhair ginger tabby, played Holly Golightly's loving cat, "Cat," or "poor slob without a name." For that role, he won a PATSY (Picture

Animal Top Star of the Year), a now nonexistent animal version of the Oscars. Orangey, whose name was later changed to "Minerva" to sound more eloquent, won another PATSY in 1962 for his role in *Gigot* with Jackie Gleason.

Orangey's career was launched in 1951 by movie animal trainer Frank Inn. Frank also trained Benji and basically laid the groundwork for modern movie animals. When he brought Orangey to his first casting call, the cat's name was neither Orangey nor Minerva; it was Rhubarb, because, well, his first movie was *Rhubarb*, and he was the star of the screwball comedy.

Inspired by newspaper headlines of millionaires leaving everything to their cats when they die, *Rhubarb* is about a sports team owner who passes away and leaves his fortune (including his baseball team, the Brooklyn Loons) to Rhubarb the cat. The players raged at the news, but it turns out Rhubarb is good luck, and he leads them on a winning streak. On screen, at least.

Off screen, Rhubarb, Orangey or whatever you want to call him, was said to be "the world's meanest cat" by a studio executive. He scratched, bit and spit on whatever or whoever he could. He was reserved in between takes, but the second the cameras started rolling, he'd wander off the set, disregarding the cost of film and production time. And then someone would have to go out and find him. His behavior was so rash that Frank

Inn had to set guard dogs at the studio exits to keep the punk on set.

And the trouble didn't end there. According to Pauline Bartel, author of *Amazing Animal Actors*, Orangey is not one cat, but many. She said that Frank Inn used several similar cats to play the same character. Like meta-acting, the cats acted as the actors. Maybe Inn was pressured to do it because Orangey, or whoever the cat was now, was a hazard to filmmakers. One thing is for sure; no matter how prestigious he may have been, he could have used a few tips from the subjects in the next story.

A Princess for the People

Movie actors shoot over to Los Angeles to launch their careers. Broadway actors dance and sing their way to New York or London. Models dream of magic in Milan. Country music artists gallop to Nashville. But when you're an itty-bitty kitty cat with so much talent, where do you go? In the case of Princess Kitty, she took her talents to a random stranger's front door in Fort Lauderdale, Florida. The random stranger was Karen Payne. On one regular day in 1986, this unforeseen encounter would eventually launch both their careers.

Karen heard a noise funneling in from her patio. When she opened the door to investigate, her mysterious noisemaker ran past her feet and scurried inside. Just like that, the feral cat thought it could move right in. No lease, no rent—she wanted a new home and she was going to take one. But she was very cunning in her choice of squatting locations. Karen had just lost her Siamese cat, Sheba, seven months earlier, ending their 13-year bond. Naturally, she missed the company of cats.

The malnourished half-Siamese kitten that entered her home had a little dark spot on her mouth that looked like lipstick. She gazed at Karen with her blue-green eyes, and Karen gazed back into hers. It was love at first sight...at least for Karen. For Princess Kitty, it was something else. When Karen approached to pet her white and brown fur, Princess Kitty bit her hand. Yup, she was a biter. Karen was ready for a kitten but not a biter. So as much as she liked the kitten, she had to show her the door.

Princess Kitty hung around the neighborhood for a few days, playing with the children and egging on the dogs. Perhaps it was all an act to convince Karen to let her move in again. After all, there was Karen in the window, clearly admiring her from afar. Karen adored the cat's spunk and spirit, and one day, she finally gave in. She walked outside, picked Princess Kitty up and made her family.

But if Princess Kitty was serious about living with Karen, she had to learn a few general house-keeping rules. The first was no biting allowed. Karen purchased a book on training cats, hoping

Princess Kitty, "The Smartest Cat in the World"

❧❀❧

to find something about keeping her new cat's teeth permanently out of her skin. She learned how to speak Princess Kitty's language. "Imitate mother cat," said the book. So whenever she was bitten, Karen hissed at her and gently pushed her nose with an open palm. Princess Kitty, who would one day be billed as "The Smartest Cat in the World," absorbed the information quickly. She was a quick learner, certainly faster than anyone had imagined.

Karen turned her new cat book into a curriculum, and Princess Kitty graduated within four months. She learned how to stay, come, sit and play dead, sometimes all within one 10-minute teaching session. Secondary school consisted of such drills as entering and exiting the cat carrier, which were taught with visual and audible cues on Karen's part. Finally, there was post-secondary school. That's about when Princess Kitty displayed exceptional talents and excelled beyond belief.

Karen devised new tricks for Princess Kitty that mimicked natural feline behaviors. For example, she taught Princess Kitty how to play the piano by using the natural instinct cats possess of pawing at dangling objects. After several months of searching for an instrument small enough for the cat to use, Karen waggled a mini conductor's wand above a mini keyboard on a mini piano, and when Princess Kitty pawed for the wand, she hit a note. Note after note she hit. It's unlikely that Princess Kitty knew what she was doing. She was just in it for the reward—garlic-marinated chicken—for doing whatever the nice lady wanted.

The cat learned to play any song that Karen conducted and that was compatible with the toy piano, as long as she got her poultry. She played "Mary Had a Little Lamb," and performed "Happy Birthday" to herself for her second birthday. But it was "Three Blind Mice" that would become her signature song. Karen need only give Princess Kitty the first couple of notes; the tune would register with the cat and she'd finish the song on her own. Even when Karen introduced a set of chimes to change things up, Princess Kitty paralleled the piano keys to the chimes, figuring out "Three Blind Mice" on the new instrument. "She actually liked the chimes more," said Karen.

Princess Kitty learned to do just about anything for a little garlicky chicken. She'd fetch a rubber ball for it; she'd dunk a miniature basketball through a miniature hoop; she'd take photos; she'd jump hoops and hurdles; and she'd give a little kiss for it, too. Soon, she didn't need food to understand it was trick time. She and Karen built such a rapport that all Karen had to do was lower herself to the floor, and Princess Kitty hypothesized that she should jump her trainer, thus inventing one of her own tricks.

The tricks eventually became less about the pleasure of food and more about the pleasure of performing. It astonished animal behaviorist Alan Beck of Purdue University. "What I like about Princess Kitty is that it looks like a good relationship," he said, "—not like Clive Beattie controlling a lion, but like Abbott and Costello working together, with the trainer as the straight man. Princess Kitty and Karen provide a model of good, wholesome humor. It's funny, and you get the impression that they are both having fun."

In just one year, Princess Kitty mastered 30 tricks. By the end of her career nine years later, she performed about 100. She never forgot a trick—sometimes doing it two or three years after the last practice—and she loved to perform. So the question was, what to do with such a talented cat?

A PBS crew was in Fort Lauderdale to film segments of *Living With Animals*. When Princess Kitty's veterinarian, Dr. Ronald Stone, learned of this, he immediately thought of Karen and company. Karen didn't believe her cat was extraordinary. She thought any cat could figure this stuff out with stringent training. "Ask the television people what they think of her," said Dr. Stone, knowing what their response would be.

The day after the producers of *Living With Animals* learned of Karen's cat, a camera crew arrived at her home, ready to roll. And thus, a star was born. It wasn't long before her name changed from Princess Kitty to "Princess Kitty™."

Princess Kitty got an agent, a headshot and some gigs at children's hospitals and schools. Every trick drew loud applause, which did not frighten her a bit. On one occasion, Princess Kitty was reluctant to perform because, like all entertainers, she occasionally wasn't in the mood. Karen took her from behind the curtain and showed her the cheerful children awaiting her show. It gave her the boost she needed, and she strutted out there and had a perfect performance.

"She loved to make children happy," said Karen. "She basked in it."

Of course, it wasn't all about the children. Some of the limelight was reserved just for her. Princess Kitty modeled for over 75 shots, and she even got a role playing Ernest Hemingway's favorite cat, aptly named Princess, in a 1988 TV biopic of the famed writer. Princess Kitty charmed Stacy Keach, the actor portraying Hemingway. Like Hemingway, Keach also had several cats—11 to be exact. Perhaps his playfulness was only appreciated by his own pets, because when he pinched Princess Kitty's tail, she hissed at him. The incident was captured on film. The director loved her "acting" and used that moment of spontaneity in the final cut.

Even though Princess Kitty was never asked to slam-dunk, wave or play a tune on the piano, she was applauded by the crew for her cooperation and patience; not once did Princess Kitty make the director call "Cut," and she never needed a second take.

Neither the Emmys nor the Golden Globes recognized Princess Kitty's role, but others did. Partly because of her talents, and partly because Karen, a former journalist, was a savvy marketer, Princess Kitty can be found on the cover of *The Wall Street Journal* and inside *Newsweek*. Pulitzer Prize–winning writer Edna Buchanan even covered the cat's birthday for the *Miami Herald*. Her roles on- and off-screen were finally awarded the 1988 "Best Animal Star" by *South Florida* magazine.

But, as Karen said, it was her role in the schools and hospitals that she and Princess Kitty felt was most rewarding. After every show, a stampede of tiny hands desperately wanting to pet her swarmed the stage.

One girl even offered to trade her pup for Princess Kitty. Another girl, smitten by a show, wrote to the famous feline. The girl's letter expressed disenchantment with her own kitty after meeting Princess Kitty. Princess Kitty wrote back, kindly advising the girl to stand by her cat with compassion and care, because all that mattered was that her cat had a loving companion.

That little piece of advice birthed Princess Kitty's fan club, the first fan club for a cat—not even Morris the Cat could top that. Although most of the 85 members were children, the president was an elderly woman who was arguably Princess Kitty's biggest fan, and any chance she had, she would be at the Princess Kitty show.

With her trainer's help, the cat got her own advice column in *People & Pets*, and they produced a training video, *Incredible Cat Tricks Starring Princess Kitty*, in which she strutted her stuff on the beach and at a costume fitting. The pair authored a booklet titled *Princess Kitty's Incredible Cat Training Tips* (by Princess Kitty as told to Karen Payne).

Sadly, the videos and books were released post-humously. In 1995, Princess Kitty died. She had gone to the vet for a minor surgical procedure and lost her life to an act of malpractice. Her death was reported on the front page of the *Miami Herald*. Understandably, Karen was devastated. She urges all pet owners to learn everything they can about their vet. "I urge them to get informed about grief [as well as] learning to cope," she said.

Karen lost more than just a business part-ner—she also lost a friend. For a long time, she could not bring another cat into her home, but when she finally did, the kitty had some big shoes to fill. Karen has already taught the newcomer,

Cat-toid

A cat spends 30 percent of its life groom-ing. That means an indoor cat, living an average life span of 16 years, will spend close to five of those years licking itself.

Countess Catlin, a few tricks of the trade. The problem is that Catlin doesn't like to show off her skills. Karen said, "She lacks the personality to perform in public."

"To find another cat like [Princess Kitty] would be an almost impossible task. [She] was a God given gift."

The Most Famous Cat to Never Live

Once upon a time, an old Parisian died and left his youngest boy nothing but a cat named Puss. Unlike the boy's brothers, who inherited a mill and donkey, the boy could only think of one use for his inheritance: dinner.

But using his wits, Puss convinced the boy that if he was supplied with a bag and some boots, he'd make the boy rich. With his utilities, Puss trudged through the woods and cajoled foolish rabbits to jump into the bag. Puss then took his meat to the French King and set it at his feet as an offering.

The King was very impressed by the meat Puss provided. Puss acted modestly, giving credit to his owner, the boy, whom he told the King was named Marquis de Carabas. The King sent the mysterious Marquis a sack of gold.

Over the months, Puss repeated his schemes. He collected more game and delivered more gold. On one occasion, while offering his hunt to the King, he overheard the King's servants arranging plans for his Majesty and his beautiful daughter, the Princess, to take a carriage ride by the river. Puss returned to the boy and convinced him to take a bath in the river.

As soon as the boy dipped his head beneath the surface of the river, Puss snatched his clothing and hid them in the forest. The cat dashed to the road and found the King, the Princess and their servants traveling as planned. Puss told them Marquis de Carabas was drowning. The King darted to the river and "rescued" the boy from the water.

When the boy realized that it was the King who held his nude body, he fainted.

Embarrassed by the boy's nakedness, the King draped him in his royal robe. He carried the boy to his carriage and ordered his coach to take the boy home, which Puss lied and said was a manor—a manor owned by a changeling ogre who, on the cunning request of Puss, changed into a mouse and was gobbled up by the cat.

Of course, like all fairy tales, it ends happily. The boy marries the princess and joins the royal family. He lives a rich life with his lovely wife and is forever indebted to a conniving, yet helpful feline.

Puss 'n' Boots, as adults know him from the fairy tale, and as today's youngsters know him from *Shrek*, is the original clever cat. His story was first told 500 years ago in many variations, but the most popular one was by Charles Perrault, who also wrote *Little Red Riding Hood* and *Cinderella*.

Although the story's overall message is actually a negative one—that it is better to make gains through trickery than hard work—it does illustrate many of our beliefs about cats. Founded on many feline traits such as independence, wit and playfulness, Puss 'n' Boots is the inspiration for many modern-day cat characters. Without Puss 'n' Boots there would be no Garfield, no Felix and no Pink Panther. His cunningness and deceptiveness outdate even the Cheshire cat of *Alice in Wonderland*.

Although he never struck a major picture deal with Walt Disney, Puss 'n' Boots was revived and revitalized as the wooing, sword-wielding kitty in the *Shrek* sequels. And in 2010, he will get his own movie, finally, with Antonio Banderas returning as the voice behind this macho cat.

~❊~

Cat-toid

In Lima, Peru, a cat named Nicolasa gained a reputation for catching waves. Although most cats detest water, this one rides on owner Domingo Pianezzi's surfboard.

CHAPTER EIGHT

Paws with Power

CATS CAN GET AWAY WITH so much more than we can, on account of being small, furry and tailed. There is a myth about a cat named Muezza from the time he spent with Islam's founder that reveals the power cats have over us.

The prophet Muhammad was sitting on the floor, and the cat was sleeping on the sleeve of his robe. He heard the call to prayer—or *muezzin* (possibly the origin of his cat's name). Muhammad was going to get up to leave for ablutions and prayer, but being the great respecter of animals that he was, he didn't want to disturb the cat. He took out his knife and cut the sleeve from his robe, slipped his arm through it, and left it on the ground, like a mattress for Muezza. Muhammad went to the mosque. The cat was exempt from prayer and slept happily into the night.

Edward Lear, the famous 19th-century English poet and artist, once had a cat that owned him more than he owned it. He was so fixed on pleasing his tabby, Foss, that when he moved to Italy, Edward had his new home constructed exactly like his old home so as not to distress the cat in its new environment. Lear couldn't afford to have a confused kitty. His cat was his muse and inspired many illustrations, as well as one of his most popular limericks, *The Owl and the Pussycat*.

Yes, some people with power yield it all to their pets. Even the most authoritarian leaders can treat their pet cat better than they do people. Consider Mime, a black and white kitty living in a Chinese restaurant just 50 yards from Windsor Castle. Although her owner is a 69-year-old common man, Mime gets the royal treatment. Since 2003, Mime has made a daily routine of dining with royalty.

She slips out of the Chinese restaurant and crawls to the castle. She is invited through the gates by the royal guard, trots to the royal apartments and lunches with none other than Queen Elizabeth's famous corgis. Afterwards, she finds her way back to the restaurant and sleeps in front of the fireplace. When castle tourists eat at the Chinese restaurant, her owner, Mr. Lam, finds himself explaining to them time and time again that, yes, "She is actually my cat!"

Upon their first encounter, things between Mime and the royal hounds—Emma, Linnet, Holly and Willow—were rough. With all the howling and hissing, woofing and wailing, it looked as if Britain would be plunged into another war. But after some appeasement from the animal caretakers, the corgis and the cat got their meals and made amends. Nowadays, Mime is a fixture of the castle. Even on the Queen's birthday, she was let in through the locked Henry VIII gates, unlike all other unannounced guests, who were sent away.

Imagine you are strolling through the King's gates and wandering toward the Queen's apartments. How long would it be before you're fired at, tackled and restrained? Shrink to one-tenth of your size, grow some whiskers and crawl on all fours, and you can apparently waltz right by, and get fed too! What a double standard.

Mr. Lam said that Mime will not eat his leftovers, but it doesn't bother him too much. He's achieved royalty vicariously through his kitty.

Fat Cats

In Pasadena, California, in 1914, a red tabby's wealthy owner bequeathed it $1000 (the equivalent of about $21,000 today). The cat's owner, Nellie Ross, wanted to be sure that the cat enjoyed its favorite dish, kidneys and cream, three times a day, or more if desired. She also left $75,000 to her relatives, giving them incentive to look after the tabby.

You don't hear about it often in the news, just often enough to know that it happens from time to time—rich people die and leave a substantial amount of their estate to their pets: a trust fund, stocks and bonds, a house or some cold hard cash.

It's enough to make us jealous, and even a little bit angry.

A cat can get by on $20 to $30 per month, but the average adult needs about $2000 just to live comfortably. That means when you adjust for "kitty-flation," Nellie Ross' cat inherited 2.1 million cat dollars.

Hellcat and Brownie, however, really hit the jackpot with their inheritance of $415,000 each. Their owner, Dr. William Grier of San Diego, died and left almost $1 million for his cats to share. And that was in the 1960s. Today, their total wealth would be over $4 million.

In 2004, the British newspaper *The Sun* published a list of the world's 10 wealthiest pets. What's scary is that Hellcat and Brownie even didn't top the list. They didn't even come close; in fact, they were at the very bottom of the list. The richest cats in history are Ani and Pepe Le Pew, worth $6.2 million each. Unsurprisingly, the richest pet in the world is a dog, Gunther IV, worth $372 million. For what? To chew on the bones of King Tut?

Several films have parodied this trend. *Rhubarb*, starring Orangey from the previous chapter, was about a cat that inherited a baseball team. A 1986 movie, *The Richest Cat in the World* included a talking cat worth $5 million and kidnappers who wanted to filch his fortune. The last Garfield movie, *A Tale of Two Kitties*, put Garfield together with a cat that inherits a kingdom from a queen. And of course, his adversaries try to take it all from him.

It's All About the Benjamins

As silly as these story lines may sound, they are just satirizing something sillier—real-life fat cats. One of the first reported cases in North America was in 1905. Once billed as "the world's richest cat," Blackie was one of Pennsylvanian entrepreneur Benjamin Dilley's two heirs. The businessman was known for four things: a successful real estate enterprise, charitableness, eccentricity and an unwavering love of cats. When he died, he left Blackie and Pinkie $20,000 each (about $470,000 today), along with his 12-room, two-story home above a cigar store—a home that was especially designed to accommodate his pets.

The interior of Benjamin's home had fixtures for felines everywhere. In all the doors, save the ones leading outside, a cat flap was installed. The furniture was always pushed to the walls to make for more playing space in the center of the room. He decorated his home with feline photography and, in each room, there were custom-made wicker baskets that on bright days were placed in a spot of sunlight for the cats to bask in. If the cats chose to sleep on his bed, Benjamin would rather sleep on the couch, so as not to disturb them.

Although Benjamin was childless, his cats were like his grandchildren. When he and his disabled wife went to Atlantic City to their summer cottage, a skinny stray wandered in. The gentle cat showed love toward Mrs. Dilley, and so her husband took it home with them to Pennsylvania to keep her company. He would always cherish the cat for the comfort it gave his wife in her dying days.

Mrs. Dilley lived long enough to witness the birth of three beautiful bouncing kittens: Blackie, Pinkie and Baby Dandy. After Mrs. Dilley died, Benjamin took to the kittens as if his wife's spirit lived within their whiskers. Each year, he took them to his Atlantic City summer cottage, just as he had done with his wife. He fed them special food that he learned they liked through experimentation. Once, he fed them boiled chestnuts. It turned out they loved boiled chestnuts, and that became their new treat. Another time, he fed them shrimp. Well, they loved that, too. From then on, the cats ate fried shrimp every Friday in summer and canned shrimp on Friday in winter.

With his wife gone, Benjamin embraced the cats as his family. Each night when Benjamin got home, he'd find the cats waiting for him on the lobby stairs. He made a regular routine of playing with the cats before bed, often staying up to "talk."

Once, he tried to take a family photo. It was a disaster. The flash bulb frightened the cats and sent them running to the walls and under the furniture. The photo was never successfully taken, and Benjamin decreed that no photos of his cats were ever to be taken.

But Benjamin was not a grouchy man. He was said to have the biggest heart in Wilkesbarre. A philanthropist, he donated money to many charities and less-fortunate people. If you were well off, you could still experience his generosity firsthand by simply showing a genuine interest in his family.

Unlike the old phrase, the way to *this* man's heart was not food; it was his cats. In his will, Benjamin made sure that reporters who wrote a blurb on his cats were rewarded $200 for every verse. He groomed and trained the cats regularly and always invited friends over to see their progress. One of these friends, Addie Ruch, loved them just about as much as Benjamin, and she would become the cat heiress.

It was a provision in his will that for $75 per month, Ms. Ruch would attend the cats in their home like a hired mother. She would feed them their Friday shrimp, make sure their bed baskets were always in the sunshine and protect them from flash photography. If Ms. Ruch died, then the executors of his will, Judge F.W. Wheaton and Walter S. Biddle, were to locate a next-to-perfect caretaker.

By the time that Benjamin Dilley passed away, it was just Blackie and Pinkie left. When Baby Dandy died, Benjamin mourned for several weeks. But the esteemed entrepreneur was happy to have the company of the remaining cats, consoling him in the same way they had done with his wife, to the last moment.

Shortly after the inheritance was partitioned, more sadness struck the family. Pinkie developed throat cancer and had to be euthanized. Although the executors agreed that Pinkie's share of the fortune would be redistributed to Blackie, it did nothing to cheer up the lone kitty. After his sibling's death, Blackie took to wandering aimlessly. From floor to floor, room to room, basket to basket, he always looked for Pinkie. He spent his last years in Ms. Ruch's lap, blankly staring back at her.

After Blackie died, the building was sold. At the request of Benjamin, $5000 was allocated for a public fountain "for the use of human beings, animals and birds."

Benjamin Dilley was a little obsessive, sure, but he was a generous man. That's more than what could be said for Anna Morgan of Florida, 90 years later.

Don't Tinker with My Money

In 1993 Anna Morgan willed $500,000 to Tinker, her Turkish Angora. Sadly, Anna didn't leave a thing for her surviving sister. Instead, a paid caretaker maintained Tinker's apartment until his day came. As Tinker was already 11 years old at the time of his inheritance, you must wonder, what happened to the money after that? Who knows? However, I'm sure Anna's sister was happy to poke fun at the cat when a decade later, another cat named Tinker inherited almost twice as much.

❦

Margaret Layne of London, England, was in her late 80s when she invited Tinker into her life. The loneliness of old age created a heavy yearning for a companion, any companion, in any warm form, as long as it made the last days of her life just a bit more tolerable. Margaret never had any children, and most of her relatives and friends were deceased or unreachable. All she had was her husband, but after he passed, too, Margaret didn't have close contact with anyone, only the occasional visit with her neighbors, Ann and Eugene Wheatley, also in their old age.

Seeing the happiness that their cats brought them, Margaret decided to adopt a kitty of her own. Serendipitously, Tinker, a black stray, wandered into her life. Not much is known about their friendship other than it was a strong one. It had to be, because when Margaret died at 89, she left a hefty trust fund and her entire estate to the little black kitty. Overnight, Tinker became the United Kingdom's richest feline. Margaret's will, bequeathing Tinker's fortune, was published in *The London Times*.

During the months before her death, the Wheatleys looked after Margaret and Tinker until Margaret entered a nursing home, at which time they just cared for Tinker. They didn't mind because

they were cat lovers, too. Acknowledging the kind-
ness with which they treated Tinker, Margaret left
the Wheatleys £25,000 (nearly $50,000). Their cut
was probably used to soften them up a little before
asking them for the big favor: to be the trustees of
Tinker's £100,000 trust fund and maintain his
£350,000 home—a total worth about $850,000.
Not bad for a once homeless cat.

And the Wheatleys kept their word, even
though Margaret's stipulations allowed them to
easily take advantage of her wishes. Margaret
wrote that if Tinker were to run away from home
and never return, the entire inheritance was to
go to the Wheatleys; if Tinker died, the money
would also be theirs. And if after 21 years Tinker
and the Wheatleys were still alive, the couple
could have it all, and presumably Tinker too. (The
Wheatleys, at the time well into their 70s, will
most likely not be alive. The 21-year limit is
strictly because of a British law that caps pet
inheritances.) Indeed, there were many ways in
which Ann and Eugene could have easily
snatched up the inheritance. They wouldn't even
have had to put Tinker down or fake a runaway.
Margaret made it clear in her will that the "trustees
shall at their discretion be entitled to bring the
trust to an end."

Instead, they kept their promise and looked
after Tinker. Although the money, which was
mostly in stocks and shares, was worth much

less after a dip in the stock market, the Wheatleys still maintained the home, keeping Tinker's environment safe. Every day they came over, filled his food and milk bowls, and on occasion, made sure he dined on his favorite food—fish.

They even let some of their own cats move in with Tinker. Although it wasn't suggested in Margaret's will, she would probably have approved of any companionship for her kitty. Margaret knew the effects of living alone. The Wheatleys introduced new flatmates, Lucy and Stardust, to Tinker. The three felines lived together like the family Margaret never had.

But trouble loomed just after Margaret's will was published and the story became an international sensation. Threats started pouring in, Eugene Wheatley told the media. Although there is no evidence of such incidents, he said people "jealous of his money" were responsible for the death threats (directed toward Tinker, not Ann and Eugene). The risk for Tinker's life was so high that they allegedly moved him to a safe house. When he was asked where, Eugene responded, "I dare not say."

Interestingly, the relocation of Tinker wasn't announced until two years after the story of his inheritance first trickled to the media. Why did the Wheatleys wait so long to reveal that Tinker wasn't living in his home anymore? It might just be Tinker's dinner, but I smell something fishy.

The Perfect Gift for the Perfect Gift

Tinker—wherever he is—is not the richest living cat in the world. Around the time that Tinker was forced into hiding, another case arose of a cat inheriting his owners' fortune. In Ottawa, Ontario, a cat inherited an estate worth $1.3 million after his reclusive owner died.

Obviously, any human who leaves their life savings to a non-human is going to be an eccentric one. But David Harper was more than just eccentric. His neighbors remember the quiet, 79-year-old man, and his mischievous three-year-old friend, with fondness and fascination. David worked as a gardener for the city's Central Experimental Farm. In summer, his 100-year-old house was decorated with flowers, but otherwise it contained only basic necessities. He spent very little money because he had only himself to look out for. He lived single and died single; there was no widow or orphan to leave a cent for. Even as a bachelor, he hardly treated himself. He was a man with a strict, stingy way of life, which enabled him to accumulate considerable wealth over his lifetime.

He ate the same supper every day: a piece of chicken and two vegetables. Every shirt, sweater and sock on his body was purchased from the Salvation Army. Every morning, he took his 5:30 AM walk around the neighborhood. And every walk was accompanied by a familiar feline.

Over the decades, a cat named Red accompanied him on his early routine. But Red is not the world's longest living cat. Hardly. He's the world's richest cat who happens to be the successor to a dynasty of orange tabbies always named Red. The Red who inherited David's wealth was given to him for Christmas, when the previous one died. The lonesome gardener cried about his deceased cat to Lynne Hammond, so she cheered him up with another orange tabby.

David and his heir lived together for about a year, until, like Tinker's owner Margaret, David became ill and had to move into a hospital. While he was hospitalized, his friend and neighbor, John Bell, looked after Red, even though Red was a brat in the past.

On their walks, David always led and Red always followed. Sometimes Red climbed up Mr. Bell's stoop and teased his dogs behind the front door. Red wouldn't meow or purr, scratch or hiss; he'd just sit there, happily hearing the dogs bark fiercely. Then he would trot down the stoop and continue on his journey with David.

John Bell didn't mind caring for the cat, but he was concerned for Red's mental health in the absence of David—or the absence of anybody at all. He felt that Red was losing his sanity in the home alone. He voiced his concerns to Lynne Hammond, the woman who gave Red to David. They both decided that Red needed an able companion, and his owner was too sick to request one, so Lynne contacted her good friend Elizabeth Butler, another animal-loving neighbor, who was happy to take Red in.

As David's lung infection and senility overtook him, his lawyer stepped in to make a crucial decision. David had already instructed his lawyer to bequeath his $1.3-million estate to Red, but he never laid out plans for how the cat would be looked after. Since Elizabeth was already fostering Red, and they enjoyed their time together, David made a deal with the United Church of Canada. After David died, his inheritance would be granted to the church, but with one condition: they had to pay for Red's expenses for the rest of his life.

Just as David had done when he was alive, Red lives a modest life on $80 per month. Food and additional veterinary costs are looked after by the church, while Red stays with Elizabeth in the same neighborhood he grew up in. As for Elizabeth, John and Lynne, they're just happy that Red is still around the same part of the city, carrying memories of their favorite neighbor on the fur of his back.

⋙◆⋘

Obviously, the people in these stories took their cat love to an extreme, but nonetheless, they thought they were doing the right thing for their favorite companions. When we die, we want our pets to have the best life possible, with the best caretakers, the best food and the best home. But I'd like to suggest an alternative to this kind of feline zealotry. Give your money to a humane center, just as Doane Randall Broggi did. The elderly woman from Orange County donated $1 million to a local cat shelter because why feed one cat when you can feed dozens?

The Mayor Maker

Little Dick Whittington of 15th-century Gloucestershire, England, had been an orphan for so long that when he shut his eyes and tried his best to visualize his parents' faces, he couldn't. He was 10 years old. He'd never been to school. He'd never owned a dime. So he packed what little belongings he had and headed for London, a city that he heard had roads paved with gold.

When he got there, he found the roads were actually made of dirt, and dirt was about all he was offered by people when he sought employment. From door to door, shop to shop, garden to garden, Dick asked, then pleaded, then begged for a job. All the grownups tilted their heads downward, cocked their brows, glowered at the boy and shook their heads.

Exhausted, Dick staggered through the city looking for something to eat until he collapsed on the stairs of a modest house. In the morning, he received an unusual wake-up call; a cooking lady was poking him with her wooden spoon, trying to shoo him away. Groggy, Dick arose and yawned.

From the second-story window, the landlord, a merchant named Fitzwarren, was watching his cook harass the poor boy. Fitzwarren called for her to cease, and the kind man invited the child inside. Dick told Fitzwarren his story—that he was a penniless orphan without a job or home. Fitzwarren was so moved by Dick's story that he gave him a room, or rather, a rodent-infested pantry to sleep in.

After finding a job shining shoes, Dick took his very first penny to a street merchant and purchased a cat named Tommy. Tommy was a magnificent cat. He and Dick became close, and he was relentless with rats. One by one, Tommy picked off the rats in the pantry, until Dick's room was rat free.

One day, Fitzwarren rounded up Dick, the mean cook and his other servants and announced to them that he was leaving London for the Orient on a trade exchange. He allowed them to choose some of their possessions to send away with the ship, which he would trade and sell for them. All Dick owned was his Tommy, a stellar ratter. Despite needing Tommy to fight off the infestation in his room, Dick sent the cat off with Fitzwarren, hoping it would pay off.

But months passed and Fitzwarren still hadn't returned. Impatient and desperate, Dick gave up on his city dreams and headed back to Gloucestershire. He'd only gotten as far out of London as Highgate Hill, when he heard the church bells ringing his name. "Turn again, Whittington, thrice lord mayor of London."

Dick hurried back to Fitzwarren's home to find his landlord waiting gleefully. Fitzwarren told him that Tommy was an incredible cat. So incredible was the feline that the King of Barbary paid him pounds of gold and jewels for the cat who rid his castle of rodents. Fitzwarren dropped a bag of riches at Dick's feet.

With his wealth, Dick was able to buy himself a home, invest in his own trading business and eventually become mayor of London.

True story? Hardly. Dick Whittington was really a mayor of London, but he was neither a poor orphan nor a cat owner. He was the son of Sir William Whittington, the Lord Mayor of another town, so he actually had politics pumping through his blood. He served four terms as mayor of London, in 1406 and 1407 and again in 1419 and 1420.

How Tommy—sometimes a talking cat—came into play is a mystery. The legend began in a pantomime version of Whittington's story and was popularized in a 1605 play, "The History of Richard Whittington, of his lowe byrth, his great fortune." Some believe that the cat myth came from the word "cat" as a colloquial term for "boat." Others believe that it came from the French word *acheter*, meaning "to purchase."

The story is a derivative of a Persian fairy tale about an orphan boy who sets his sights on India to gain wealth and finds success with the help of a phenomenal mouser. Although the legend is too antiquated to bear any truth, one thing is for sure—Tommy has stuck with the story of Dick Whittington. A 17th-century engraving of Whittington by Renier portrays the mayor with a cat, and on Highgate Hill, the Dick Whittington Stone is capped with, what else, a cat.

Discounting Muezza belonging to the Prophet Muhammad (who some do consider a political figure) Tommy may be the first powerful cat to have political ties. But he most certainly was not the last.

Chief Mouser to the Cabinet Office

The exceptionally furry, black and white London stray wandered into Downing Street. The humans around him bustled across the streets and parks, dressed in sharp suits and dresses, hands full of locked leather suitcases and humungous 1980s mobile phones. He scampered past their glossy shoes and through a gated fence. On the other side, the October lawn was the color of an unripe banana, but it was impeccably mowed and well kept, just like the hedges in the area.

In front of him was a big, brown brick building soaring higher than the rest. His instincts told him somewhere inside there would be food and, more importantly, warmth to alleviate the fall chill. A sturdy man in a black vest, holding a gun and wearing a large black hat, stood beside the door like a statue. He paid the cat no mind, so the cat did the same to him.

The stray lurked before the door, waiting for another suit to open it up and either invite him in or give him ample opportunity to slip inside. He did not have to wait long. The busy building had comers and goers entering and exiting at a dizzying speed. When the time was right, the cat slipped between the legs of someone exiting the building. He gazed around the opulent lobby at the shiny ornaments that indicated plenty of wealth. *Jackpot*, he thought.

He wandered the hallway mazes searching for a mouse, but every time a human spotted him, they wanted to touch and stroke him, or pick him up

Cat-toid

Some ruthless dictators and demagogues have more in common with each other than just their tactics; they also share a hatred for cats. Adolf Hitler, Napoleon Bonaparte and Julius Caesar could all be classified as ailurophobics. However, Sir Winston Churchill, Pope Benedict XVI and Abraham Lincoln were passionately fond of cats.

and ultimately get in the way of his feast. Finally, he couldn't take it anymore. He scampered away and tried to find himself an empty room. Although he couldn't find any with open doors, he did find a room of people too busy talking and leafing through papers to notice him. He crept inside and watched.

One of the women was particularly interesting to observe. While most of the people around her were men, it was she who stood at the head of the table, dressed in a rose red pantsuit. Her pearl earrings looked like delicious fish eyes, and the puffy red hair on her head looked like smoked salmon. And then, when he looked at her eyes, he found them looking right into his. She got up from the desk and approached him, cornering him helplessly. She stretched out her arms and kneeled down. She slipped her hands under his tummy and lifted him up to get a good look at his face. He considered scratching her, but he imagined that any harm to a person of her importance would have dire consequences.

"Hello," she said. "My name is Margaret Thatcher. What's your name?"

Well, he didn't have one, not at the time, anyway. Maybe before their serendipitous meeting, he did have a name, but now that he was a stray, he was without one. So he was given one: "Humphrey," as in Sir Humphrey Appleby, the fictional civil servant in the British sitcom *Yes, Prime Minister*.

Okay, so it wasn't actually Prime Minister Thatcher who found Humphrey; it was an unknown Cabinet employee. But it was Mrs. Thatcher who let him stay.

Only two years before Humphey wandered in, about the time he was born, the building's previous mouser, Wilberforce, had died. Wilberforce resided there for 15 years, and with him gone, there was a serious mouse problem that needed fixing. So from the day Humphrey entered the building, he had a home. He was allocated £100 of annual tax money for food and litter, and given the title Chief Mouser to the Cabinet, a position that dates back to King Henry VIII. His legacy spanned three prime ministers, for a total of eight years, and as with so many politicians, ended in scandal.

He didn't have a very complex job, but it was a big one indeed. His job as Chief Mouser was not just limited to that one building; it included the entire Downing Street area with all its confusing, twisting roads. He made his own hours and had no quota to fill. As long as he kept the rodent population down—which he did very well, and at a price thousands of pounds cheaper than the hired exterminator who had not once caught one mouse—Humphrey had a career.

From Prime Minister John Major's Cabinet, a 1992 memorandum described Humphrey as "a workaholic who spends nearly all his time at the office, has no criminal record, does not socialize a great deal or go to many parties and has not been involved in any sex or drugs scandals that we know of." Another memo released the next year announced that, after a veterinary check-up, Humphrey had bad kidneys and should therefore not be fed any treats.

And the following year, more problems arose, not from his health, but from his alleged gruesome murder of four robin chicks nesting on the window-sill of John Major's office. The prime minister came forward the day after Humphrey was slandered, saying, "I am afraid Humphrey has been falsely accused."

In 2005, a dossier obtained under the Freedom of Information Act by the *Daily Telegraph*—the same media that made the initial allegations 11 years earlier—said of the accusations, "This was a libellous allegation and was completely unfounded." This was at a time when Humphrey, a gentle-natured cat, had been ill with kidney trouble and sleeping for most of the day. He could not have caught anything even if it had been roast duck with orange sauce, presented on a plate.

Perhaps Prime Minister Major was a bad influence, because a year after the "Robin-gate" scandal, Humphrey was in the news again, this time, as a runaway. The impetuous moggy disappeared and was presumed dead. After three months, the Cabinet's press office announced his death to the public. The pronouncement inadvertently led to the discovery of Humphrey at Royal Medical Army College, where staff and guests dubbed him "PC."

Through the press, Humphrey released a statement upon his arrival, saying, "I have had a wonderful holiday at the Royal Army Medical College, but it is nice to be back and I am looking forward to the new parliamentary session."

Humphrey took a year off from causing any outrage in 1996, but in 1997, his final year as Chief Mouser, he was the catalyst for Tony Blair's biggest political controversy prior to the Iraq War.

Mrs. Cherie Blair, the new prime minister's wife, was known for two things: her shoe collection and her strong aversion to cats. She found them unhygienic. When she and the family moved into Number 10, within one week, talk of Humphrey's exile was afloat. The British paparazzi unleashed a campaign against Mrs. Blair so damaging that the First Lady had to take a photo op to clean up her image. Posing on the Number 10 lawn, Cherie Blair hugged Humphrey in her arms for the cameras. It's hard to tell who looks more nervous, Mrs. Blair or Humphrey.

The two cohabited for just seven months when, in November 1997, Humphrey's caregiver said the cat needed to retire as Chief Mouser because his kidney problems were worsening. Humphrey required a "stable home environment where he can be looked after properly." But the announcement of his Downing Street removal was not made public until the day after his relocation. The reasons for the delay were to avoid "would-be catnappers," the caregiver said.

The media, and the Conservative opposition, weren't buying it. Conservative MP Nigel Evans claims that Humphrey was leaving in protest of the Labour Party's exemption of tobacco advertising. He said, "Humphrey clearly can't stand the stench of hypocrisy which reeks from Downing Street after the 'donations for exemptions' affair." He also added, "Perhaps, like all other groups who have suffered from Labour's broken promises, he didn't get the loving attention he was promised in May from the new occupants of Number 10."

There were also more destructive rumors suggesting that Humphrey was not relocated but was put down on the orders of truth-spinner Alastair Campbell for defiling the Blairs' rug with urine. The accusations were so virulent that the new Labour government organized a media campaign at an undisclosed home where Humphrey now lived. The press photographed Humphrey as though he were a hostage, standing upon the Monday morning newspapers to prove he was indeed alive. And yet, it wasn't enough to absolve Cherie, Tony, Campbell and the Labour Party.

It was pretty obvious that Mrs. Blair prompted Humphrey's removal. Number 10 was supposed to find a replacement Chief Mouser after the ailing cat moved out, but about 10 years would pass before another moggy was appointed to the Cabinet. Sybil came in as Humphrey's successor, but only recently, in September 2007, after the new prime minister, Gordon Brown, and his family moved in.

Humphrey's official death was announced on March 20, 2006. If this is true, he lived a prestigious 18 years and will be known as the most famous Chief Mouser to ever scurry the Downing Street area. That is, of course, until Sybil stirs up a royal storm. She's got some big paws to fill.

Pussycats on Parliament Hill

Canada has always had an emphatic reputation for offering itself as a place of sanctuary for travelers, immigrants, refugees and expatriates. My own parents immigrated to Canada 30 years ago to escape the hardships in Lebanon, pre- and post-civil war.

If you hike up Parliament Hill in Ottawa, take the trail behind the Peace Tower and above the Ottawa River, and stomp through some trees and bushes, you'll find a community of rescued cats living in a replica of the Centre Block of the Parliament Buildings, a symbol of Canadian amnesty.

These cats receive as much support as all newcomers to this country do. They have access to universal health care—including vaccination and treatment by an Ottawa animal hospital. And they also...well, actually, on second thought, they don't work half as hard as do immigrants, or any Canadians for that matter.

They get free food and toiletries, all provided for by personal donations. They also get to live in their own little house in the mock Parliament block. They can roam wherever they want, past the gates, and even inside the Parliament buildings. Of course, when let inside, the cats are expected to help exterminate the rodents (and no, I'm not talking about your least favorite Member of Parliament). Actually, some of the cats are rumored to have descended from earlier mousers of Parliament Buildings.

The "Cat Sanctuary" building is the handy work of René Chartrand, a jovial 83-year-old man who constructed it himself. (He built and maintains the cats' home, and feeds them twice a day, sometimes from his own fridge.) René, a retired house painter and Quebec native, moved to Ottawa and overtook the project in 1987, after Irène Desormeaux, a woman who cared for strays on Parliament Hill in the 1970s, died. In many ways, Irène is the Cat Sanctuary's founder.

Currently, more than 25 cats live there. The area is enclosed by a fence, which is opened at night so the cats can leave, but is kept secured in the daytime to protect the tourists. As cute as they are, René acknowledges their wildness.

The Humane Society of Canada gave him the Heroes for Animals Award in recognition of his

Canadian Prime Minister Stephen Harper in his office with two foster kitties

dedication, but René just does it for the love of cats and visitors. "It's fun to meet the girls and boys and senior citizens," he told the *Canadian Press*.

In addition to René and Irène's project, there is another humane effort in Parliament, this one supported by Prime Minister Stephen Harper. He and First Lady Laura Harper are avid participants of the Ottawa Humane Society's foster program. At any given time at 24 Sussex Drive, you may find several shelter cats snuggling with the Harpers. They foster several kittens with health and behavioral issues. And when those cats overcome their problems and are adopted out, the Harpers generously take in more.

"My family and I are animal lovers and deeply value the companionship of our pets," said the prime minister. "Unfortunately, and all too often, some family pets such as dogs and cats find themselves in shelters as a result of being abandoned or rescued.

"My family is proud to participate in the Ottawa Humane Society's Foster Program by opening our home to cats in need of foster care."

Who knows, your cat might have government ties.

Purrers at 1600

President Harry Truman once said, "If you want a friend in a Washington, get a dog." It seems that for most American presidents, that advice still rings true.

The White House is no stranger to dogs. American presidents and their pups are about as noticeable as the building itself. Going as far back as the original founding father, George Washington, presidents have had canine companions, possibly because dogs are viewed as masculine archetypes, whereas owning a kitten would be seen as "soft." Since the building's construction, only a handful of cats have found a home at 1600 Pennsylvania Avenue.

Abraham Lincoln was the first to bring home a cat, a little critter named Tabby. Obviously, considering the atmosphere of the Union and

Confederacy, not much attention was paid to Tabby, and so not much is known about the cat.

The cat belonging to the19th president, Rutherford Hayes, was not only the first cat in the house in 13 years but also the first Siamese cat in the United States. Siam, as the cat was named, was a present from the American Consul in Bangkok.

But it wasn't until Theodore Roosevelt took office that the White House cats garnered more attention, perhaps because of their personalities. President Roosevelt, a strong man who grew up as an ailing boy and defied his physical limits, was virile enough to win a war, yet tender enough to inspire the first Teddy Bear. His affection for Slippers, an avid relaxer, reflected Roosevelt's gentleness, whereas Tom Quartz, a feisty fighter, reflected his strength.

Slippers was a polydactyl cat, and this was apparently enough to put him above everyone else. Slippers had access to important meetings, sitting at Roosevelt's side, purring happily as the president and his administration discussed national defense and peace between Russia and Japan. At a momentous 1906 diplomatic dinner, the president was hosting current leaders of the world. Slippers snuck into the function and promptly fell asleep on the rug in the hall between the lobby and dining room. As President Roosevelt led the leaders to dinner, they stepped around the royal cat, admitting their inferiority.

Tom Quartz, a kitten named after a Mark Twain character, was a skittish battler, which President Roosevelt found very amusing. He often wrote about Tom Quartz in the now famous letters to his children. The kitten attacked just about anything it saw, striking fear into Roosevelt's dog Jack, who, the president wrote, was once chased by Tom Quartz for five minutes before hiding away in shame.

In a letter from January 1903, President Roosevelt wrote to his son Kermit, "Tom Quartz is certainly the cunningest kitten I have ever seen. He is always playing pranks on Jack, and I get very nervous lest Jack should grow too irritated." He then went on to tell a story in which Tom Quartz stealthily attacked the Speaker of the House's leg and then made a downstairs dash.

President John Kennedy's children, Caroline and John Jr., introduced Tom Kitten to the White House, though his stay was shortened by the president's allergies. President Jimmy Carter's daughter Amy brought home the unfortunately named Misty Malarky Ying Yang. The Siamese cat was the last feline resident at the White House until the Clintons moved in from Little Rock, Arkansas, and brought little Socks with them.

The First Cat

"Socks" was very much Chelsea Clinton's kitty. Chelsea discovered Socks in 1991— when daddy was just a governor and presidential hopeful—on her way to piano class. The previous year, the family's cocker spaniel Zeke was run over and killed. Her parents decided not to get a new dog so soon because they felt Zeke was irreplaceable. But when she saw Socks and his sibling Midnight roughhousing in her piano teacher's garden, Chelsea wondered whether a cat applied to the new-pet restrictions. Fatefully, Socks was as enamored by Chelsea as she was by him. When she reached down to pet him, he jumped into her arms and thus became a Clinton himself.

The kitty is mostly black, with white smears across his face and down his belly and white paws that give the appearance of socks. He moved to the White House from the Arkansas governor's mansion shortly after papa Clinton took office. President Bill Clinton and First Lady Hillary Rodham Clinton both were very fond of Socks. For five years, Socks remained the undisputed "First Pet." He was made into a little celebrity, posing for pictures in the oval office and the press room, while his cartoon understudy guided website visitors on a virtual tour of the White House.

Socks was mostly an indoor cat. The Clintons didn't want a repeat of what happened to Zeke, so when he was allowed outside, Socks had to be leashed. Still, it didn't keep him from preying on squirrels and birds, like all cats should. He even made a friend, a stray tabby called Slippers (after

Roosevelt's polydactyl). The two distant cousins often shared food and water. When he did retreat inside, Socks had a luxurious, three-story cathouse to hang out in. It was built by one of his many fans.

He was a big hit overseas, too. The Central African Republic released nine stamps featuring the presidential pussycat. He was immortalized in two books, *Socks Goes to Washington: The Diary of America's First Cat* by Michael O'Donoghue, and *Dear Socks, Dear Buddy: Kids' Letters to the First Pets*, edited by the First Lady.

Socks, like most cats, had a carrier that he traveled in. However, unlike other carriers, this one had the presidential seal. The First Lady often took him to functions at nursing homes and schools, and once out of the carrier, the docile kitty would lounge in her lap, under the strokes of her palm, purring throughout the meetings. And unlike Humphrey, his only controversy was using White House stationery to respond to the letters of children, a fact disputed by Republican Representative Dan Burton.

Socks' luxurious lifestyle was torn apart when the inevitable happened: the Clintons decided it was time for a new pup. In 1997, Buddy, a Labrador retriever, moved in and began his campaign to impeach Socks. Socks resented his presence immediately. When they met for the first time on the White House lawn, Socks hissed, Buddy barked, and the president had to break up the scuffle. Hillary Rodham Clinton said of their first encounter, "[Socks] despised Buddy from first sight, instantly and forever."

Socks could hardly be blamed. Every time he swiped at Buddy, it was in self-defense. Buddy got his kicks from chasing Socks around. And too quickly, Socks' custom-made carrier was left to gather dust as Buddy was taken aboard Air Force One for vacations and diplomatic meetings. When the press asked President Clinton how the two pets were cohabiting, he said they were "making progress." In another interview before his departure, President Bill Clinton said, "I did better with…the Palestinians and the Israelis than I've done with Socks and Buddy."

Predictably, when it was time to leave office, only Buddy went along with the First Family to New York. Socks stayed in Washington with Presidential Secretary Betty Currie.

Two years later, Buddy was dead, struck by a car like the Clinton's first dog. Socks could not be blamed, for he was hundreds of miles away. But perhaps he possessed some extraordinary abilities? Could it be that he telepathically guided the wheels of a van over his nemesis? As you will read in the next chapter, some felines claim to have some pretty freaky powers.

CHAPTER NINE

Freaky Felines

SONYA FITZPATRICK IS A PET PSYCHIC. Actually, she is *The Pet Psychic.* The show, which once ran on Animal Planet, was in the same vein as many of the cold-reading psychics, such as John Edwards and Sylvia Brown. Fitzpatrick welcomed pet owners to the show along with their pets and used her supposed psychic powers to speak with the pet, learn what irked them, provide counseling and pass the message on to the owner and television viewers. Or so she claims.

Here's how a typical segment on her show might go.

Fitzpatrick: How do you feel when your owner leaves for work and doesn't come home until late?

Cat: [Nothing.]

Fitzpatrick: And do you think that's fair?

Cat: [Nothing.]

Fitzpatrick: So what would you like done?

Cat: Meow.

Fitzpatrick's obvious advantage is that we can't translate the animal's sounds, and besides, she claims that they speak to her telepathically. Her supposed talents are nothing extraordinary, and neither are the pets she brings on, she claims. In her book, *Cat Talk: The Secrets of Communicating with Your* Cat, she said that everyone is capable of making "cat talk." You just have to try harder, apparently; but really, you need to deceive yourself—at least just a little bit. If you are rarely home and your cat is unhappy, you need not speak with your cat, telepathically or otherwise, to know that you need to take a moment and assess your relationship.

Fitzpatrick takes her claims one step further. Segments of her book are allegedly written by cats and transcribed by her. (Not surprisingly, all the cats seem to write in the same style as hers.) But pet psychic therapy aside, is it possible that our cats have paranormal powers?

In "Traveling Tails," we looked at reported cases of psi trailing, a phenomenon yet to be confirmed or invalidated. There is much to be said for animals' extrasensory perception—much we don't know about and much we are incapable of knowing about. Can cats really predict natural disasters? Can they sense when a companion is returning home? Are their senses limited to ordinary animal instincts, or do they have powers that we don't have or have yet to learn?

The January 2001 issue of *Your Cat* tells two stories of extraordinary psychic cats. The first is that of Elisabeth Bienz, a Swiss woman who moved to Paris and left her cat behind with her parents. Shortly afterward, Elisabeth's cat ran away. But every few months, when Elisabeth returned to Switzerland for a visit, the cat would mysteriously meet her at her parents' home. After Elisabeth flew back to Paris, the cat would vanish again. One day, the cat showed up at the parents' house on a day when Elisabeth was still in Paris... or so her parents thought. As it turns out, Elisabeth was coming home for a surprise visit.

The other story included in *Your Cat* was that of a cat named Godzilla and his owner David Waite of Watlington, England. Mr. Waite was a traveling businessman, constantly in and out of the city and country. His parents would frequently cat-sit Godzilla while David was away. Checking up on his parents and cat, David would occasionally call the house at random hours and on random days. Amazingly, Godzilla would always run next to the ringing telephone when David was on the other end of the line, or so his parents reported. Godzilla ignored the phone whenever someone else was calling; he only paid attention to it when his beloved owner called.

Of course, there is no way of validating these claims. It's possible that David's parents only remember Godzilla's "hits," disregarding or forgetting about his "misses." The same thing could be going on with Ms. Bienz's parents. It's possible that they just weren't looking out for the cat and therefore didn't notice when it returned on days that Elisabeth did not visit.

Paranormal researchers Pamela Smart and Rupert Sheldrake, a biologist, published a report in the *Journal of the Society for Psychical Research* showing that a great many pet owners believe their cats and dogs have psychic abilities. While only 14 percent say their cats can predict when they are coming home, 48 percent say that their cats know when they are about to leave the house, even before the owner provides visual cues such as putting on a jacket or reaching for keys. One-third of the subjects believe their cats communicate with them telepathically, responding to thoughts and silent commands.

Claims of cats and other animals "predicting" natural disasters, especially earthquakes, is well documented in history. Ancient Greek historians noted a case in 373 BCE when the city of Helice was shook by an earthquake; just days before the earthquake struck, the animals had evacuated the city.

In a 1994 case in California and a 1999 case in Greece and Turkey, Sheldrake reported testimonies of people who witnessed their cats nervously hiding well before the quakes.

According to Roni Jay's *The Kingdom of the Cat*, in 1944, a kitty named Toto helped rescue his family from a volcano. The cat lived with a couple in Italy. One night, Toto's human father awoke because Toto was being aggressive, scratching at him and biting his cheek. Toto's owner tried to stop him, but Toto was persistent. The wife, a superstitious woman, believed that the cat was trying to tell them something. Because they lived so close to Mount Vesuvius, an active volcano, she concluded that it could erupt, and they had better get out of the area before it did. After she convinced her husband, they packed what they could and got out quickly. Not an hour later, their house was smothered in lava and ash, and 30 of their neighbors were dead.

Jay also writes of another Italian case, in 1976, when people living in the Friuli district noticed cats running amok around town, scratching and hissing and meowing, and, overall, acting like lunatics. It wasn't just the feral cats either; the house cats were doing it, too. As soon as their owners opened an outside door, the cats would try to make a run for it. Hours after the feline riots, a major earthquake struck the region.

The best reported case of animals "predicting" impending earthquakes was in 1975. The day before the quake, citizens of Haicheng, China, noticed irregular behavior in their cats and other pets. What they witnessed was so alarming that seismologists advised the citizens to evacuate the city. Because people paid attention to the animals' behavior and took the signs seriously, thousands of lives were saved.

But before naming your cat Scientist of the Century, you must also consider that a year later in China, an earthquake struck Tangshan and killed over 200,000 people. Neither the cats nor the seismologists predicted that tragedy.

Believers suspect that our pets pick up on variations in electromagnetic fields, and the sudden change makes them frantic. Similar to the cases of animals foreseeing their owners' arrival at home, the quake claims have yet to be confirmed or discredited. The United States Geological Survey says that animals cannot be used to predict earthquakes. On their website, they assure people that animals "change their behavior for many reasons, and given that an earthquake can shake millions of people, it is likely that a few of their pets will, by chance, be acting strangely before an earthquake."

❧◆❧

Ernest Bozzano is a world-renowned parapsychic—one of the first in his field—who spent the first half of the 20th century studying psychic phenomenon until he died in 1943. He was a lover of animals, and he believed that he and his cat could communicate using extrasensory perception (ESP).

Bozzano claims that when he was at his work desk late one night, he dropped his pen, sensing that his cat was in danger. He arose from his seat and searched the house from top to bottom, looking for her. There was no sign of her. He stepped into his yard and searched his grass and garden. In the darkness he heard a hollow meow and followed the sound.

He found her caught in a rabbit snare, still alive, but had she made any sudden movement, she wouldn't have been. He believed that because he responded to her silent pleas, he was able to save her.

Bozzano's cat must have been a very vulnerable and clumsy one, because on another occasion, he had to help her out of his attic. After he and his family did an exhaustive search for the feline, with no luck, Bozzano channeled visual flashes of his attic, and that was where he found her. He claims that he always keeps his attic closed. It's a freaky story even without the telepathy. But is it true?

One way to tell if your cat is psychic is to check if it is left- or right-handed—that is, according to Dr. Joseph Rhine, researcher of the psi trailing phenomenon. He said that of his cat subjects, "truly psychic cats are often left-handed." So how do you figure out what hand orientation your cat is? Do you gesture to shake a paw and see which one it offers? Do you give it a pen to see which paw it writes with? Maybe you could hand it a fork and observe which paw it grabs the utensil with?

It's quite simple, actually. Long, but simple. Offer a piece of food to your cat, but don't put the food in a place where the cat can eat it without lifting a claw. Make them use their paws. Put it in a tube or somewhere they'd have to reach into. Then observe which paw they use. Record it and do it again. Repeat until a dominant paw becomes apparent. If it's the left paw, it's possible the cat already knows what you're thinking. And it's probably thinking something else, too: "This is the easiest dinner I've ever had!"

The ancient Egyptians believed that cats had divine powers as a whole, but the first individual feline suspected of possessing unworldly powers was believed to be Satan incarnate. He was the catalyst of evildoing in the very first witch trial of the 16th century. In many ways, he is the original freaky feline.

The 16th-Century Killer Cat

This story is an interpretation of the facts stated in "The examination and confession of certaine Wytches at Chensforde in the Countie of Essex before the Quenes majesties Judges, the XXVI daye of July Anno 1566," the first-ever witch trial.

In the small Christian village of Hatfield Peverel in 1541 lived a little girl, maybe age 12, named Elizabeth. She looked up to an elderly woman,

Mother Eve, as a spiritual guide. One day, Mother Eve told Elizabeth the ways of witchcraft as if it were an antiquated version of the "birds and the bees." She taught her spells and curses and told her about spirits and cats. The knowledge was never meant to turn Elizabeth to the dark side, but rather, to help her get a leg up as a young woman in a patriarchal society, using untapped sources from unseen spirits. Finally, Mother Eve gave her Elizabeth a one-year-old white cat to get her started. The ominously named cat, Sathan, was the Easy Bake Oven of spirit familiars: all you needed to cook up a wish was to place him on your lap, pet him, give him a drop of your blood and ask him to provide.

The cat, according to Elizabeth, not only drank blood and realized wishes, but he could also talk. At first, the human-like mews were unintelligible, what Elizabeth later testified as being a "strange hollow voice." But with time, translation and plenty of practice, the cat's creepy communication came to fruition.

She kept Sathan, perhaps out of fear or loneliness, but as she aged into womanhood, she struggled to provide for herself and the cat. So she fed Sathan some blood and wished for sheep. The next day, Elizabeth found 18 sheep feeding in her field. Elizabeth was befuddled, and so were the people of Hatfield Peverel.

Her neighbors thought she was lucky, until, within a week, the sheep died. Sathan's shoddy wish fulfillment occurred again and again. First, Elizabeth wished for a rich, handsome man and got one, only to realize he was a complete jerk, who impregnated her, then refused to marry her. She fed Sathan a drop of blood so that he would fix her problem, and Sathan not only rubbed up against the man, causing him to drop dead, but also gave Elizabeth the scoop on a potion that could abort her baby.

Elizabeth wished for another man. One who would love her and provide for her emotionally, not just financially. A man who would marry her. Along came Christopher Francis, an honorable agriculturalist. Three months later, Mr. and Mrs. Francis welcomed the birth of a beautiful baby, though the neighbors cocked their brows at the sudden birth. But Elizabeth struggled as a mother. She couldn't meet the baby's demands, and one night carelessly wished the child would shut up. Sathan realized this wish without the usual drop of blood. Elizabeth regretted it immediately.

After the death of their child, Christopher and Elizabeth bickered constantly. She couldn't take it anymore. She asked Sathan to paralyze Christopher, and the cat complied.

Poor again, Elizabeth resorted to trading whatever she had for whatever she could get, including Sathan. Wrapping the cat in an old apron, Elizabeth delivered it to her neighbor, Agnes Waterhouse, in exchange for a cake. Just as Mother Eve had once instructed her, Elizabeth told Agnes to prick her finger, give the cat a drop of blood and make a request. Elizabeth then returned to her lame husband, hoping the truth about her past never caught up with her.

Mother Waterhouse was an innately despicable woman and couldn't wait to test Sathan. It wasn't long before she had the cat kill a man named William Fynee. Afterwards, Agnes and Widow Gooday, a neighbor whom she despised, got into another of their regular quarrels. Agnes had Gooday's cow and geese drowned. Her vengeful acts and obvious malevolence unsettled her neighbors, and she was accused of being a witch. To hide the evidence of Sathan, Agnes had him turned into a toad. That was the last time the cat was seen.

Elizabeth Francis, Agnes Waterhouse and Joan Waterhouse, Agnes' daughter, stood trial on charges of witchcraft written out in the Witchcraft Act, passed only three years earlier. The women confessed to their murders and spells; however, the judges seemed to sympathize more with young Elizabeth and Joan. Whereas Mother Waterhouse was hanged two days later, Elizabeth was only sent to prison for one year, and Joan was acquitted.

It's important to remember that, as with almost every witch who was tried and condemned, their confessions came under torture. It is possible that these women were pinning blame on the cat with a colorful name to avoid being hanged. Christian superstition associated cats with evil, so the women's shared feline was an easy scapegoat. Unfortunately for Agnes, she had a terrible reputation with the community, and therefore the court had no compassion for her.

After her release from prison, Elizabeth Francis was feared in Hatfield Peverel. She was a favorite scapegoat when anything was amiss, and it wasn't long before she was sent back to prison, and to the pillory four times, for bewitching another neighbor. Seven years later, she was accused again, but this time, she was sent to the gallows.

As for Joan Waterhouse, she claimed that her talking dog was responsible for the death of her 12-year-old neighbor. A dog that responded to the name "Sathan."

Had these women and Sathan come from Prestonpans, Scotland, their names would now

Cat-toid

Some historians believe that the rampant spread of the black plague could have been stymied if it weren't for the superstitious slaughtering of cats. While cats in Europe were rounded up for their apparently satanic relations, their prey, rats, flourished and spread the plague.

be cleared. In 2004, on Halloween day, the town pardoned 81 alleged witches and their cats, who were executed more than 400 years ago. That is just 81 out of the approximately 3500 people and cats killed for superstitious reasons.

The Grim Sleeper

The Steere House Nursing and Rehabilitation Center in Providence, Rhode Island, is a place surrounded by death. People with few days left on their calendars come to the hospice to die as comfortably as possible. While the human instinct is to run away from death, one extraordinary staff member at Steere House actually runs to it. Oscar, a two-year-old cat with chubby cheeks and a perpetually solemn face, lives on the third floor of the hospice and has an extraordinary tendency to point out the next death in the dementia ward.

Since Oscar moved in, he has predicated the deaths of over 25 patients. Of course, Oscar doesn't just check up on the patient and announce his diagnosis to doctors. His technique is more subtle and interpretative.

Oscar paces the east and west wing of the dementia ward, freely entering the rooms and always using his nose. He trots into a patient's room, hops up on the bed and sniffs them. He ruminates over the scent and then either hops off the bed and wanders on to another room or sits down and snuggles with the patient. If he does the latter, the nurses take notice and begin the procedure of notifying the patient's family.

No, she is not tattling on the cat for his invasion, nor is she calling to ask the family if the patient is allergic to cats. She is calling them to inform them that their loved one has only a few hours to live. Because Oscar has such an outstanding record, the family will usually rush to the hospice and proceed with a prayer and vigil. Usually, the family welcomes Oscar's presence until the very end, believing that his company consoles the dying. If he is not welcome, he is removed from the room. When Oscar is excluded from the vigils, he patiently waits outside the door until the patient takes his or her last breath, and then he leaves. However, this claim is not supported by the *New England Journal of Medicine* (NEJM), which first disclosed Oscar's role at the hospital.

Dr. David Dosa published the article, "A Day in the Life of Oscar the Cat," in July 2007, after the geriatrician noticed that over six months, Oscar's seemingly random routine was not random at all. "He doesn't make too many mistakes. He seems to understand when patients are about to die," Dr. Dosa told the *Associated Press*.

But Dr. Steven Novella, a neurologist, and president and co-founder of the New England Skeptics Society (NESS), thinks otherwise. He believes the claim is a case of confirmation bias, which is "the tendency to make and remember observations

that confirm a belief we already have," according to what he wrote in his blog, NeuroLogica.
He hypothesizes that all it took was a few instances
of Oscar cuddling with a dying patient to alarm
nurses. The nurses were probably captivated by
what they witnessed and spread their observation
throughout the hospice. With that precedent,
everyone at the hospital started looking for corre-
lations between Oscar's company and the patients'
deaths. And thus, the possibly random occurrences
make for paranormal convictions.

"No one will much notice, report or remember
the times Oscar visited a patient and they did not
die soon after," said Dr. Novella.

Believers often cite the fact that Oscar's case was
published in NEJM as incontrovertible evidence.
But it's important to note that the article was not
peer-reviewed and was simply a doctor's perspective.
Not even Dr. Dosa confirms Oscar's grim instincts.
Dr. Novella calls NEJM's publishing of the article
"an error in judgment on their part. It is likely that
they felt this was little more than a curiosity, a cute
human interest story."

Another hypothesis is that Oscar can smell
chemical changes in a dying person's body that are
too subtle for people to detect. It's possible that
Oscar is just reacting to the smell. People who
believe this more scientific hypothesis still think
Oscar is sticking around with the dying out of
empathy. If the metabolic-smell idea is true, then

it's also possible that Oscar is sticking around because he likes the smell. Obviously, that's not as pleasant a thought, but it is possible. (I mean, I once had a cat that smelled my feet a lot, and so far, I have not developed athlete's foot.)

Steere House staff and the family of their patients, however, are mostly convinced that Oscar is trying to tell them something with his super cat senses. Oscar is known to be an aloof creature, even more so than most cats. He's considered to be very antisocial and self-absorbed, more interested in his next meal than his next client's therapy session. The hospice has five other cats, a rabbit and many birds, all of which are typically more social than Oscar. Yet only Oscar has displayed such mind-boggling behavior.

Whatever stimulates his actions, Oscar is admired by Steere staff, patients and their families. At the entrance of the dementia ward, a plaque on the wall reads: "For his compassionate hospice care, this plaque is awarded to Oscar the Cat."

My Pet Ghost

If the claims about Oscar are true, then we know that cats can predict death. If the myth about Sathan is real, then we can conclude that cats can cause death. But what do we know about cats that can see death after the fact? Many ghost-believers think that cats and other animals have a sixth sense for spotting the undead.

Benjamin Radford, a scientific paranormal investigator (not to be confused with new age paranormal investigators, or ghost hunters), has a very special tool he uses when investigating an allegedly haunted area: cats. He introduces a feline to the suspected room or home, monitors the cat's reaction and moves on from there. "I like to use cats whenever I can," Radford explains. "They don't eat too much!"

More often than not, the ghost detector will gently rub its furry head against Radford's leg and beg to be petted. When that happens, it's basically saying, "nothing to see here." He usually uses the case subjects' cat, not his own, Zevon. "She hasn't chased any ghosts with me," he said, adding optimistically, "maybe one day when she's older!

Radford doesn't actually believe that cats can see anything significant that we can't already see, but he uses the cats to reassure pre-set believers. "It's just a matter of trying to debunk people who assume that any cat reactions must mean something... 'They' say in ghost circles that pets and young children are especially sensitive to ghosts. Is there any proof of this? No. But people (mis)interpret animal reactions to fit their expectations." That may be so, but what about cats that don't see dead people at all—but see dead cats instead?

Deb Richardson had two rambunctious kitties: Itchy and EDKSky (short for Evil-Demon-Kitty-Sky, a name Deb's husband insisted on). The two cats were a handful, but there was no one they terrorized more than each other. They often played "stalk the kitty," in which one of them (usually EDKSky) would sneak up on the other, pounce and make its opponent hiss and scram. Then the other would retaliate with the same shtick. Back and forth, they'd stalk and chase each other. "They could keep it up for ages!" said Deb.

One day, upon returning home with her husband from his dad's funeral, they learned of yet another sad death. While they were gone, the cat sitter opened the door, and Itchy made a run for it. She was never heard from again. In her absence, EDKSky began acting strangely. Actually, he was behaving just the same, but without Itchy, it was quite peculiar.

EDKSky would crouch and creep up on an invisible figure, pounce and chase whatever it was that he was after, and then, just as if Itchy was returning the favor, EDKSky would hiss and act as though he was being chased around the house. Deb said that it wasn't just a one-time instance; EDKSky would often play stalk the kitty alone, as if Itchy had never left.

"Now," said Deb, "when I see EDKSky playing stalk the kitty all by himself, I say hi to Itchy, just in case she can hear me."

❧◆☙

Unlike Benjamin Radford, Sue Darroch is a paranormal investigator who *is* a believer. She'd have to be—she saw a ghost cat with her own eyes. Not long after she and her spouse moved into their new home, they found signs that they were not alone, or at least, not without a pet.

One evening, shortly after the move had begun but was nowhere near being finished, Sue entered the house and was startled to see a cat dart across the hallway floor and into another room. Sue followed its trail but found nothing at the other end. She first assumed the cat was a neighbor's or a stray, but no doors or windows provided the mystery cat with a way in. So she then assumed it was a trick of light mixed with her own exhaustion from the big move.

She put it behind her until one week later, when her husband informed her that he'd seen a black and white cat posed on the kitchen stove. He said that he quickly turned his head, checking for an open entrance. He didn't see one. Even weirder, when he looked back, the cat was gone.

Her husband's sighting was not the last. On another occasion, a guest asked them about their cat. *What cat?* thought the couple. *Oh…that cat.*

Cautious with her assumptions, however, Sue classifies all three eyewitness accounts as "subjective." It's her job to view the paranormal through an objective lens; she is the director of ParaResearchers of Ontario, a non-profit organization that investigates paranormal claims and offers expertise on such subjects.

Although the aforementioned cat is the only personal animal apparition she's encountered, Sue said that they are not as unusual as you might think. In fact, from experience, she's found approximately an equal amount of animal and human apparition claims. "The most common reported to us would be a household pet," said Sue, adding, "[Cats and dogs are] the most frequent."

The organization cannot investigate every claim because most are retrospective cases filed years after the first and (usually) only instance. But whenever possible and permissible, she and her team of investigators will open a file. "All natural possibilities are looked at first. If we cannot explain the event, it then becomes what we believe is an anomaly."

As for what the ghost cats want, Darroch admits she hasn't the slightest clue. "My own speculation [is] they seem to be no different from their 'human' counterparts." She said that whatever the reason any ghost appears, it's more mundane than media and movies would like us to believe. "I like to think that because ghosts and animal apparitions in general have been reported for hundreds of years, 'they,' whatever 'they' truly are, are a natural extension of the human experience."

True or not, you've got to admit, ghost cats are a lot more cost-efficient than their tangible relatives. Other benefits include not having to clean the litter box, or have a litter box at all, not having to vacuum cat hair off the couch before your friends arrive and not having an allergic reaction whenever they're around.

Guardian Angel

For Leslie Boyce and her family, finding Allie was like uncovering a lost treasure. Actually, Allie was not lost at all; he was abandoned. Someone in La Crescenta, California, didn't see the value in the white kitten, and they dumped him in the mountainous woods by Leslie's house.

Allie's life with the Boyce family was a quiet and humble one. The long, slender cat spent a lot of time stretched out on the floor, taking up more floor space than a cat really needs. He was, as Leslie said, "the most laid back cat." He liked sun tanning, but enjoyed his time in Leslie's lap even more. He had a trade-mark symbol of affection when sitting in her lap or lying on her chest; he would push his head under her chin and rub her neck really hard.

Aside from his role as a professional lounger, Allie acted like a guardian to Leslie's girls from the day they were born. Wherever the babies were, Allie would be right there with them, gently standing guard against whatever threat he thought could harm them. "He was always near them, even when I changed their diapers," recalls Leslie. "He let the little ones drag him around; he never minded."

The girls and Allie grew up together, and soon Leslie's daughters were bigger than he was. But then came an incident when Allie, who always looked out for the girls, wasn't looking out for himself.

He was outside of the house, probably lying in the California sunshine, when a coyote attacked him. The coyote sunk its teeth into Allie's stomach and pulled him so hard that the force de-clawed Allie. Although Allie managed to get out of the canine's grip and away to safety, he was never the same again.

When Leslie found him, he was bleeding profusely from a two punctures in the side of his stomach. When she first saw the abdominal holes, she thought someone had shot Allie. But remembering the coyotes that lurked in the area, she guessed again.

She took him to the vet, who did his best to repair the damage. But only so much could be done. Allie spent the months after the ordeal sick and saddened. He lost weight and became physically and behaviorally unusual.

While Allie was injured, Leslie became his guardian. During his recovery, in early 1994, the Northridge earthquake rattled the West Coast. Leslie saved him by pulling him out of the dangerous hallway and to safety.

Even after an attack by a coyote and another from Mother Nature, Allie kept on purring. But his health was waning. He must have suffered brain damage, because his cognitive functions

were deteriorating. And then, one day, he disappeared all together.

Noticing his morning absence, Leslie went into the
yard looking for him. There was no sign of Allie
there. Her search became more frantic. She took to
the deep woods and higher up the mountains—still
nothing. She looked in every place she could think
of, every bush and every trail, exhausting herself in
the process. Hours into the search, her thoughts
sobered. She thought about his physical condition.
Although it was unlikely that he could leave the
area in his wounded state, she realized that if he
had, he would be even less able to defend himself.

Leslie figured he must be dead somewhere,
either in the wilderness or in the house. She gave
up her search and got into her car to begin her daily
errands. As she turned on the ignition and pushed
the clutch, she heard a pained mewing. She turned
around and found Allie, in terrible condition, lying
limp on the backseat. He looked up at her, and she
saw that he developed an infection around his
mouth. He meowed through rotting lips. She froze,
horrified and repelled, as Allie cried for her.

Leslie regained her composure. She brought him
into the house and gave him water. Allie began to
have massive strokes, and then he collapsed and
lay quietly on the floor. He still breathed, still
opened his eyes, but cried no more. She placed
him into a comfy basket and let him rest; and he
did, with disturbing silence.

Allie lending her protection to Leslie Boyce's baby girl

⌁⌁⌁

Because it was a Sunday, the area's animal hospital was closed, so Leslie thought she would take
him to the vet first thing Monday morning. She sat
with him quietly throughout the night. By 3:00 AM,
just hours before the animal hospital opened for
business, Allie became agitated.

"He was thrashing all over and fighting to stay alive," recalls Leslie. "I knew he was already brain dead. His body would not let go."

Leslie couldn't bear to watch this anymore. She could feel his suffering, and she knew that letting him endure it any more was inhumane. She had to act. She had to do the unimaginable. She had to put him out his misery. She did so, crying the entire time.

"This was the only thing I could do. I wrapped him in blankets, and then into several plastic garbage bags. I sealed off the air, laid him back down in the basket, and put some pillows on top of him to help his body calm down from the weight, so he would hopefully give in to passing."

The next morning, Allie was buried near their home.

Over the week, Leslie felt awful. She couldn't come to terms with her actions and carried the weight of guilt everywhere she went. One day, when Leslie was home alone, she entered her bedroom, closed the door and laid down for a siesta. She thought about the precious moments of the life she and Allie had shared. She reminisced about the times when Allie would lie in her babies' cribs and sleep next to her daughters. She remembered how he would say, "I love you" by smudging his little head under her chin.

Just as her eyes were closing, she heard the clear sounds of paw steps in the room. Leslie sat up and panned the room with her eyes. Except for her, it was empty. She must have imagined it. She lay back down and shut her eyes. Suddenly, she felt the pressure of something jump onto her bed. It was a feeling she recognized from her days with Allie. She shot back up, peered down at her feet and around the bed. Nothing was there.

She pulled her body back down to the bed. She shut her eyes again, but kept herself conscious and aware. She listened intently for any more paw steps, and she kept her nerves ready for any more bed hopping. She waited and waited, and suddenly, she felt a small object materialize on her body and crawl up her chest.

And then she felt him—pushing and rubbing underneath her chin.

"This gesture let me know he was okay, that he forgave me and was thanking me. I cried, but I knew I was right with what I felt." What she felt was a rush of relief washing through her body as the weight of guilt lifted from her soul.

Leslie said that Allie's spirit visited her often, "just to say hello." On various nights, as she lay in bed, she'd hear him enter the room. She could feel his presence. "I could hear him walking on the floor but I'd see nothing there. I could, on occasion, feel a cold spot in the room and feel him get on the bed and lay down."

And she wasn't the only one. Her daughters also witnessed sightings of Allie's ghost, sitting on the washing machine or lying on the windowsill sunning himself. Even in death, Allie was still their guardian.

Over the years, Leslie and her family visited their cat's grave to talk to him. Once, while at the gravesite, they took a family picture. In the developed portrait, Leslie said that a blue orb can be seen. Leslie enlarged the photo and zoomed in on the orb. "Inside," Leslie said, "you will see a cat face."

Thirteen years later, in 2007, Leslie—now a professional spiritographer and co-founder and lead investigator of Southern Spirit Seeker Society—has rescued four cats: a mother and her three kittens. Leslie adopted out the mother and one of the kittens, but kept two at home. One of them, Atticus, has developed a peculiar behavioral trait.

"He will get up on my chest and sleep, and rub my chin with his. I looked at him one day and all I felt was this was Allie come back to me."

~∞×∞~

Cat-toid

According to *Guinness World Records*, the oldest cat ever was a 38-year-old named Crème Puff (1967–2005) from Austin, Texas.

CHAPTER TEN

Chic Kitties

CINNAMON, A FOUR-YEAR-OLD Abyssinian living at the University of Missouri-Columbia, is unlike her siblings and peers living in the same corridors. She is shy. While the other cats at the university favor frolicking, she likes to stand silently and observe. Her reticence is probably why biologists chose her to be their subject in decoding the DNA of cats to bank in the mammal genome club, an exclusive group that only has information on a handful of animals.

In late 2007, scientists sequenced Cinnamon's DNA using a "shot-gun" method of cutting up the DNA and reassembling it to find integral traits and mutations.

Purposely bred to have retinitis pigmentosa, she was born with a disorder that leads to blindness. Humans are vulnerable to the same disorder. By identifying the gene that causes the degenerative eye disease, scientists hope to someday cure retinitis pigmentosa.

And their aspirations don't end there. Of the 250 hereditary disorders that a cat can be born with, many are shared with humans, such as retinitis pigmentosa, muscular dystrophy and polycystic kidney disorder. And some diseases that cats can contract, like Feline Immunodeficiency Virus, have similar versions that occur in humans. Cinnamon's DNA could lead to medical breakthroughs previously unimaginable, both in humans and their favorite furry companions.

The first-ever scientific experiment in "improving" cats was conducted in 1885. Francis Galton, a half-cousin of Charles Darwin, and whom *The New York Times* once described as "one of the most ingenious and yet useless persons," had an unusual dream for a super subspecies of domestic cats. Did he dream to make them quicker, more agile and muscular? Did he dream of making cats more disease resistant or healthier all around? Did he dream of making super cats that don't regurgitate hairballs onto your carpet? No, the brilliant scientist wanted to make cats deaf by breeding albino kitties, who are often born deaf.

Fortunately, since Galton, experiments in creating new cat breeds have been generally benign. Many cat fanciers' favorite cats are hybrid results of experimental breeding, like Bengals (Asian leopard cats crossed with domestic shorthairs), Savannahs (African Servals crossed with domestic cats), Safaris (Geoffroy's cats crossed with domestic cats), and Ocicats (Siamese cats, Abyssinians, and American shorthairs). And there are more breeds on the way.

"What will they think of doing to us next?" thinks this cautious cat.

⚜

Ojos Azules is a breed of domestic cat that has been a sought-after gem for more than 20 years. The first Ojos Azules ancestor, Cornflower, was discovered in 1984. She was picked up because of her mesmerizing eyes, which are a deeper blue than a Siamese cat's. Yet, after all these years, cat fanciers still can't get their paws on this lovely creature because the kittens are born with too many defects.

In New York, breeder Sarah Sweet's Siamese gave birth to a kitten with strange, wooly, coarse and curly fur. The kitten became "Wooley," and his descendants, "Brooklyn Wooleys." Brooklyn

Wooleys are still in the experimental stage because so many of the kittens are born with the opposite outcome: baldness.

Some failed experiments have been abandoned all together.

The Dutch Rex was discovered in the 1980s in the Netherlands. The cat had fur similar to Brooklyn Wooleys—coarse, bristly and woolly—but as they aged, the hair roots weakened. The follicles would give up, and hair fell off the cat, leaving it with bald spots. Breeders gave up shortly afterward.

However, some breeders see baldness as a virtue. Dick and Nellie were two Mexican hairless cats gifted to an American couple by a local Native American tribe in the early 20th century. The cats, unlike Sphinxes, did possess some short hairs on their body; however, they shed in summer, and the fur would grow in again depending on the season. Their owners had high hopes for this newly found breed, but unfortunately, Dick was attacked and killed by vicious dogs before he could impregnate Nellie.

But not all experiments have been partial or total failures. Some new experimentally bred cats are already dazzling their owners. But as you will see, the price tag is dazzling too.

Honey, I Shrunk the Tiger

Tigers are one of the most fierce, hypnotic and beautiful creatures in the wild. They are also one of the most endangered. Of the six non-extinct subspecies of tiger, only about 5000 to 7000 remain. Cat breeder Judy Sudgen learned this when she was a little girl, and she dreamed of one day helping to preserve the big cat. And now, after 20 years of selective breeding, she has...sort of. She's managed to create a new kind of domestic cat that brings the safari attraction right to your sofa.

Toygers (a take on "toy tigers") are the size of domestic tabbies, but they feature striped markings around the body and on the head that give them the look of miniature Sumatran tigers. Aside from their dog-like dependency, love of water and sharp hunting skills, they're just like a regular tabby.

Judy knows the arduous process of cat breeding well. She is a second-generation breeder; her mother, Jean Mill, created one of the most sought-after cat breeds, the Bengal. Like her daughter, Mrs. Mill introduced Bengals to raise awareness of animal protection. She believed that by bringing a leopard-looking pet into people's homes, the public would be more reluctant to wear leopard furs, and therefore, reduce the spotted-fur trade.

In a secret genetics lab in Southern California, Judy, an architect, keeps her new breeds in cabins secured by wire fencing. She protects her kittens not from outside breeders (there are about 25 other Toyger breeders), but from animal activists who consider the cats unfairly treated. Judy believes that the activists aren't fully aware of her objective. Not only does she want to find these cats loving homes, but from each sale, a donation is also made to a tiger conservation charity.

The first attempt to breed Toygers was in the 1980s. Judy crossbred her mother's Bengals with a common Tabby (in that way, Toygers are truly a family business). The results weren't great, but she continued on with her pursuit of the mini tamed tiger. In 1993, just after registering Toygers with The International Cat Association (TICA), she found just what she was looking for.

On the streets of Kashmir, Judy found a stray cat with striped markings on its head, something tigers have but domestic cats don't. She took it home.

But even after all her and her affiliate breeders' efforts, Toygers are still a work in progress. Not all of the features laid out in TICA's standards have been met. By 2010, Sudgen and associates hope to have a pumpkin-colored Toyger with a white belly, and black stripes reaching up from the belly to the spine. It should be big boned and muscular compared to a regular tabby. They also hope for smaller eyes and a rounder nose and ear tips. By using computer imaging, they have model constructions of "the perfect Toyger."

In the meantime, you can buy a prototype for $1000 to $4000. It's a hefty cost, but it's outweighed by the amount you'll save on medical bills by not being mangled by an actual tiger.

Attack of the Clones

"CC" looks and behaves like a normal cat; she's curious, independent, affectionate and known to purr from time to time. But CC is an exceptional kitty, not because of her behavior (she has yet to dial 911, play the piano or predict death), but because of her DNA. CC's name stands for CopyCat, because she is a clone. In fact, she is the first cloned pet in history.

She was born practically a four-year-old, not because her immediate genetic ancestor, Rainbow, was that age—but because that's how many years it took for CC to go from test tube to kittenhood. Rainbow's second life began as a scientific and commercial venture called Missyplicity, which was funded by a billionaire entrepreneur who wanted his dog, Missy, cloned. Before cloning Missy, however, they wanted to try it on cats first.

Genetic Savings & Clone (GS&C) was hired to do the work, a gene-banking company that will store your pet's genetic makeup for a cost of more than $1000 (plus annual maintenance fees). When they started gene banking, the company's idea was to hold on to a customer's pet's genetics until the advent of cloning, but they didn't think they would be doing the cloning. As cloning information pro- liferated and people began investing, GS&C took up the task. They called it Operation CopyCat.

GS&C extracted cells from an unnamed cat- donor's ovaries, removed the DNA and replaced it with Rainbow's. A total of 87 of Rainbow's embryos were implanted into surrogate mothers, but only one budded into a full-term pregnancy. On December 22, 2001, "CC" was born. The details of her birth were not revealed for another two months. Scientists assessed her health, confirmed her success and published their findings on Valentine's day.

Soon, CC was pictured in *Time*, *USA Today*, *The Wall Street Journal* and every other major and minor newspaper on the continent. But something baffled the editors, readers and even the scientists at GS&C: CC looked absolutely nothing like Rainbow. Their only resemblance, it seemed, was being of the same species.

Rainbow was brown and white tortoiseshell; CC was a brown and white tabby. Yet an analysis of CC's DNA proved the two cats were clones. How could that be? It had to do with the mutation called X-chromosome inactivation. Not much is known about it, but it seems that one of the X chromosomes inherited from Rainbow shut itself off, and CC took one from her tabby surrogate mother instead. Skeptics found it hard to believe that CC was indeed a clone, but the discrepancy in hair color didn't silence the critics of cloning.

The Humane Society of the United States publicly condemned the experiment, stating that by cloning pets, GS&C was slapping in the face the many organizations struggling to adopt out rescued pets.

However, the Humane Society was not acknowledging the cost of cloning. Each clone costs tens of thousands of dollars, and at that rate, it could only afford to clone a few animals per year, which hardly has an effect on the vast number of sheltered pets. As Joan Miller, legislative coordinator of the Cat Fanciers' Association, said to *Cat Fancy*, "Cloning is not even a drop in the bucket."

Some scientists admit that having a pet cloned is almost pointless because clones do not inherit personality. CC and Rainbow not only look different but also behave differently. They are more like fraternal twins than clones.

GS&C continued with their exploration of cloning, but with a different scientific process. Instead of using nuclear transferring of the DNA, they used chromatin transferring. The result was five more cloned kitties, two of which had the same donor, and all of which looked just like the original cat.

The first two were Tabouli and Baba Ganoush, clones of a Bengal cat named Tahini. Unlike CC, Tabouli and Baba Ganoush were displayed to the public. At Madison Square Garden in 2004, they were exhibited at the Cat Fanciers Association/IAMS Cat Show. The clones and their donor live together in California with GS&C's CEO, Lou Hawthorne.

After another GS&C employee had her cat Mango cloned into Peach, GS&C was ready to go commercial. For a nominal fee of $50,000, they will clone customers' pets. They opened for business in 2004, but closed their doors in 2006. The reason? Not surprisingly, pet owners were not *that* interested in having their pets cloned.

GS&C only served two customers. The first was a woman known only as Julie, who had her deceased 17-year-old Main Coon, Nicky, cloned; she named the clone Little Nicky. He was the first-ever commercially cloned pet, and unlike CC and the others, his owner claims that he acted very much like his donor. GS&C's brief popularity resulted in the cloning of another pet owner's cat, Gizmo. However, Little Gizmo would be their last commercial clone.

It seems that after they proved themselves capable of cloning, there wasn't much left for GS&C to achieve. No doubt, cat owners thought it was an interesting notion to have cat duplicates frolicking together with the endearing confusion a regular cat might have with its mirror reflection. But understandably, people were slightly more interested in paying off a mortgage.

In response, GS&C slashed their price from $50,000 to $32,000. Still, nobody was willing to pour his or her hard-earned money into uncertain outcomes. GS&C shut down and transferred their customers' banked pet genes to another company. Missy the dog has yet to be cloned.

Mad Catters

Lifestyle Pets is a new league of pet store. Walk into their headquarters and you will not find cat food and kitty litter, cat nip and kitty toys, collars, treats, scratch posts—no, you won't find any of that. The only thing they sell is pets, and if you want one, the wait can take a year, and the cost is somewhere between buying a used minivan and buying a new convertible.

Lifestyle Pets employees don't wear blue and yellow vests with name tags and lanyards. They're more likely to wear lab coats, and in the offices, suits. What makes their cats so special? They are all scientifically researched, bred and monitored.

Lifestyle Pets cats first made a splash in 2006 with Allerca GD, a patented breed of hypoallergenic cats. Between 5 and 10 percent of people have cat allergies, therefore limiting how close they can get to cats and restricting them from cat ownership. But with an Allerca GD, anyone, regardless of their health, can enjoy the company of a cat without sneezing.

According to the company's website, the breakthrough was accomplished by monitoring genes of domestic cats and searching for a divergence that didn't produce Fel d 1 glycoprotein (the naturally occurring protein found in most cats' fur, mucus, urine and salivary glands); it's the same protein that triggers 95 percent of cat allergies. Once those mutant cats were found, they were isolated and crossbred, and their kittens were examined.

Next, the Allerca GD kittens were used in an experiment with people who were allergic to cats. The human subjects were put in a room with the selected kittens, and Lifestyle Pets claims that no person displayed any sinus trouble. For a control, regular, non-Allerca GD cats then joined the same subjects. The result was sneezing, scratching, wheezing and sore and scratchy throats, along with itchy, red eyes.

Even though the study was neither published nor peer-reviewed—and Lifestyle Pets keeps its information confidential—the cats allegedly are hot commodities. The kittens cost about $6000 each, and in 2009 the company plans to release a Siamese version at almost double the price. Anyone so eager to have a cat that they're willing to cough up that kind of money must harbor a cat passion comparable to that of the ancient Egyptians.

Believe it or not, Allerca GD's cost is only a fraction of Lifestyle Pets' latest endeavor, the Ashera. Named after the Syrian fertility goddess of the Canaanite civilization, this domestic cat is about 4 feet long when it's completely outstretched; it has a svelte build, and an adult weighs about 30 pounds, having more muscle than your average house cat. Its fur is marked with leopard-like spots, and, according to the company website, the cat takes well to leashes. No, this isn't some tamed big cat that escaped from a zoo into Lifestyle Pets' headquarters. It's their $22,000 (minimum, and not including $1000-plus shipping fee) breeding experiment.

Sold as the "world's rarest and most exotic domestic cat," Asheras are a hybrid of two exotic felines and house cats. Lifestyle Pets says that Asheras are a combination of African serval, Asian leopard cat and common domestic cat. Because of the cats' ancestral roots, the company recommends you provide them with a heated bed. (Apparently, they like warmth even more than your cat that is stretched out by the radiator right now.) And be sure to get them an extra-large bed, and especially an extra-large litter box.

As wild as the cats seem, Lifestyle Pets assures customers that they eat the same food and enjoy the same companionship as other cats. Their website claims that "Ashera cats are highly intelligent, very affectionate and have great temperaments." And unsurprisingly, you can get hypoallergenic Ashera GD kittens for an extra $6000.

Ordered kittens arrive at your door hand-delivered, spayed or neutered, with all their supplies and trinkets, plus a tracking microchip, one-year warranty and, perhaps strangest of all, a "Certificate of Authenticity that will include an image of each kitten's DNA 'fingerprint.'" It takes almost one year to obtain an Ashera, and like all luxuries, they're limited edition. Only 100 Asheras are sold worldwide per year.

But exactly how rare are they? Like the Allerca GD, Lifestyle Pets keeps the data on Asheras top secret, leading many cat breeders to believe that the Ashera is just a Savannah breed that has been registered with TICA since 2001. Savannahs and

Asheras are about the same size, act similarly
and look very much alike. They are both descendants from the African serval, and as Savannah
breeder Patrick Kelley puts it, "any cat bred from
a serval is a Savannah." Many Savannah breeders,
like Kelley, believe that the alleged Asian leopard
cat cross-breeding is a complete fabrication.

Kelley is the creator of the Exotic Cat Network,
and he runs the largest Savannah cat breeders' website online. He is an outspoken critic of Lifestyle Pets
and the company's founder, Simon Brodie. He tells
me that Mr. Brodie contacted him about six years
before the advent of the Ashera, proposing a business venture with genetically modified Savannahs.
The two quickly lost contact. The next time Kelley
heard about Mr. Brodie, he was marketing a familiar feline under another name.

According to *Union Tribune*, Savannah breeder
Cynthia King was also contacted by Mr. Brodie, but
under a fake name (which Brodie later admitted to
doing), looking to buy five to seven fertile, first-
generation Savannah females, each at $7000.
Again, the deal never went through. But months
later, King learned of the Ashera press material.
She immediately turned her skeptical eye to Brodie.

Patrick Kelley points to the Ragdoll controversy
for perspective. A California breeder introduced
a new breed of gorgeous, puffy cats called "ragdolls,"
claiming that the cats contained raccoon and
skunk genes. Cat fanciers were in a frenzy, eager

to get their paws on these toy-like cats. But the breed was completely unsubstantiated by science.

Kelley said that, as with Asheras, you mustn't believe all the hype. He does say, however, that the Savannah is an amazing cat in itself. "When the African serval and domestic cats first started to be crossed, there were scientists who did not believe it could be done... The two cat species are so drastically different physically." Not only that, but the Savannah's personality is not what you would expect considering its size and ancestry. "The Savannah isn't just a big cat; it also has an amazing personality. These cats are smart and are what I call aggressively affectionate. When a Savannah wants a hug, he or she just comes and gets it."

Unlike Savannahs, Asheras are not a registered breed, which gives skeptics even more reason to disbelieve Lifestyle Pets' claims. It seems that the only major difference between these look-alikes is in price; Savannahs sell for a quarter of the price of an Ashera.

Extremely Mad Catters

All cat owners have experienced that terrifying, unexpected moment when, in a dark room, you catch a glimpse of two glowing eyes floating in the darkness. Your heart skips a beat and you forget to breathe, but then you sober up and realize, "Oh, it's just you, kitty."

Imagine that same scenario, but instead of two glowing eyes, you see a full-grown fluorescent feline.

A team of scientists at Gyeongsang National University, with funding from the South Korean government, say their glow-in-the-dark cats may one day lead to amazing medical developments. Developments that can save lives, extend life spans, save endangered species and solve mysteries behind hundreds of genetic diseases plaguing primates and felines. It might be a little bit of a stretch, because when I look at pictures of these Turkish Angoras, I only see unnaturally luminescent red cats under ultra-violet rays.

But don't say that to Kong Il-Keun and his partners. They believe it's just the tip of the iceberg. "The ability to manipulate the fluorescent protein and use this to clone cats opens new horizons for artificially creating animals with human illnesses linked to genetic causes," said the Ministry of Science and Technology in an international press release put out in December 2007.

What they did, or at least what they claim they did (remember, South Korea was also the site of the human-embryo cloning scandal in 2005, which injected fellow scientists and the media with ripe skepticism), was to use a red fluorescent protein to modify skin cells from the Angora kittens' mother, and then insert the gene-modified nuclei into extracted eggs. When cloned embryos developed, they inserted them into the mother's ova. One basic, two-month cat-reproductive cycle later, and voila! The cat mother gave birth to four replicates of herself, with one difference: they glowed under special lights.

Unfortunately, one of the kittens was still-born, but the others grew to be functional, healthy adult cats.

The reason the cloning team believes this is a milestone in curing genetic diseases has nothing to do with the cats' luminescence. The glow gene is just an easily recognizable example of gene modi-fication that can be proven visually. It simply lays the groundwork for modifications the human eye cannot detect to diseases like Lou Gehrig's.

Glow-in-the-dark clones are not all that new. Pig and mouse clones have already been produced using green fluorescent proteins found in jellyfish. Pretty much any animal injected with the fluorescent protein in the embryonic stage could be produced. The glowing cats are simply the first in fluorescent pet technology.

When the glow-in-the-dark pigs got pregnant, they gave birth to little glow-in-the-dark piglets. Soon, we may have glow-in-the-dark kittens running around, too. But before you go to your local pet store seeking one of these ultra-cool cats, you must realize that they have no intention of releasing these cats commercially. And if they did, there is no guarantee that they would be permitted in all places. For example, GloFish, genetically modified fish, were banned in California.

Cat in a Lab Coat

Most cats in science are usually part of the experiments themselves, but one cat actually helped in conducting the research. He was as much a part of the study as the researchers, data collectors and article writers. The cat helped guide a researcher in learning whether or not animals are capable of achieving abstract, human-like emotions.

Most people remember Koko the talking gorilla, who lives in California and has a vocabulary of more than 1000 words, which she speaks using a derivative of American Sign language (ASL) called Gorilla Sign Language (GSL). Koko can also understand a range of human words, and she has proven her intelligence for almost 30 years. But aside from showing that animals, or at least mountain gorillas, are capable of sophisticated communication, Koko also showed that they can display empathy and feel sadness.

Living in Koko's massive shadow is All Ball, her pet kitten whom few people remember.

In the summer of 1984, Koko made an unusual request to her companion and caretaker, Dr. Francine "Penny" Patterson. Using GSL, she asked Penny if she could have a cat. It was a timely request; a litter of kittens had just been abandoned nearby. Penny retrieved the kittens and allowed Koko to choose one. From the litter, she picked a gray Manx, which researchers believe she chose because the kitty had no tail—just like Koko.

When it came to naming the kitten, Koko called him All Ball, because he looked like a furry, gray ball.

Koko and All Ball were great friends, almost family. Koko displayed her most gentle and maternal instincts with the kitten, attempting to nurse him, carrying him on her back and wrapping him in a pink blanket. All Ball was also very affectionate with his surrogate mother, often snuggling with her at night. Sadly, however, just a few months later, All Ball left the gorilla's trailer and was struck by a car. Koko would have to learn the facts of life, and it was up to Penny to break the news.

Penny entered Koko's trailer, where the gorilla sat in the corner of the room slouched and worried.

"Koko," she said, signing as she spoke aloud, "All Ball, hit by a car." Koko didn't quite understand, so Penny explained to her as best she could that All Ball was never coming back.

"Bad, sad, bad" signed Koko. "Frown, cry, frown, sad."

She cried alone for days. It was genuine bereavement—a not at all surprising discovery for researchers. Three days later, Penny went to Koko, hoping to comfort the gorilla. "Do you want to talk about your kitty?" she asked.

"Cry," signed Koko.

"What happened to your kitty?"

"Sleep cat."

"Yes," Penny nodded, "he's sleeping."

"Koko good."

Although she was only capable of comprehending death to the extent that a small child does, Koko did have a basic understanding of death—life ends abruptly, and when it does, there's no coming back.

The next year, Koko learned something else about life: there are second chances. Choosing another litter of Manx kittens, she was allowed to keep two. She named them Lipstick and Smokey.

The Inventor

Sir Isaac Newton was busy with another experiment in the attic, cutting himself off from the world, as he usually did. His only visitor was his cat, which he lived with but barely had time for. He gave her a free pass to roam around the house, as she liked, wherever she liked. On this particular day, however, her visitation rights were interfering with his scientific research.

Newton was studying the order of color in a prism. To conduct his experiments accurately, he required a controlled light setting, which is why he was in his attic and not his study—the attic had a lone window that allowed light to shine into the prism. The problem was that Newton's cat was spoiling his experiment with her constant entering and exiting of the attic. Each time she squeezed through the door, she nudged it open and let in unwanted light. But Newton felt it was unfair to banish the attention-seeking cat. After all, she didn't have much company throughout most her life.

Newton arose from his desk and put his prism-color tests on hiatus. His new priority was devising a way for her to enter and exit at will, without stymieing his studies. Using a saw, he cut a square hole into the wall, big enough for his cat to crawl through. He then cut a strip of felt and attached it to the top of the opening, so that it draped over the hole. He didn't have a name for it at the time, but people would eventually call his invention the "cat flap."

With the cat flap, Newton and his cat could work at will—he on his groundbreaking discoveries in physics, and she on her discovery of human silliness.

You see, even geniuses aren't immune to overzealous ailurophilia. When Newton's cat had a litter of kittens, the brilliant scientist didn't realize that they, too, could use the same cat flap. Instead, he cut smaller holes into his door, next to the original cat flap, to accommodate their smaller bodies.

CHAPTER ELEVEN

Your Amazing Cat Story

IF YOU'RE READING THIS, chances are that your cat has never saved you from a fire or an attacker. Aside from the odd time your feline had to be lured down from a tree or cajoled from under the furnace, you've probably never had to save your cat's life, either. Your cat has probably never spied on any Russians or fought in any wars. Hopefully your cat is neither a criminal nor a ghost. If your cat has telepathic powers, it's doubtful that they can be used for anything more than signifying when it is lunchtime. Your cat has probably never been in any movies and has probably only modeled for your Christmas card photos. You're probably not a nation's leader, and your cat probably isn't either. And unless this book is reprinted for the next 200 years, your cat is probably one of a kind and definitely not a clone.

However, though you may not already realize it, you do have an amazing cat story. By simply owning a cat—caring for it and giving it a home—you are prolonging your chances of living a long, healthy life. Much scientific data indicates that pet ownership is one of the best things you can do to maintain a wholesome life.

Experiments have found that vibrations between 20 and 140 Hz can improve bone growth, help heal fractures and torn muscles and reduce body pain and swelling. Well, a cat's purr fits within these levels of vibration, and it, too, can be therapeutic. Similar to ultrasound treatment, a cat laying on your body and purring can prove beneficial to you. Scientists are researching whether purring can even hinder osteoporosis and restore bone growth in elderly people and post-menopausal women.

A study at the University of Warwick in England found cats to be exceptional therapists. Researchers discovered that cat owners recover from spousal bereavement better and faster than non-cat owners, and that cat owners also have fewer physical and psychological health problems. Cats also provide exceptional emotional support for women with breast cancer.

You may be thinking, "Yeah, sure, cats are healthy for them, but what about people with allergies?" It's true, people allergic to cats do suffer in the presence of the animal's fur, but you have to realize that part of the reason they have allergies in the first place is because they probably weren't exposed to cats at an early age. A study at the Institute of Paediatrics and Adolescent Medicine in Munich found that children who grew up around at least one cat were 67 percent less likely to develop allergies. Another study found that children who live with cats or dogs in their pre-elementary years are less likely to have asthma or develop hay fever. (One variable not mentioned in the study, however, is why the children weren't exposed to cats early on. It may have been because of noticeable allergy symptoms realized before choosing to own a cat. Or it's possible their parents were allergic and wouldn't allow cats into the home; allergies can also be hereditary.)

A United Kingdom study by Emma Osborne found that 81 percent of children under 13 would rather disclose their feelings to their cat than their parents or a friend. At first glance, it may seem sad, and perhaps indicative of the decaying family structure, but it actually shows just how meaningful animal companionship is to children. Almost the same number in that group said cats helped them be more social, and 87 percent said they consider their cat to be a "close friend."

And it's not just children who benefit from their feline companions, either. In the same study, Osborne surveyed cat-owning seniors. She found that 62 percent of them claimed that their cats helped them cope with, or defeat, loneliness, and 82 percent said their cat helped them overcome stress. Of the same group, three-quarters said they'd rather share feelings with their cat than with family or friends. Compare that with the per-centages of children who prefer the same, and you'll see that after two generations, people still regard their cats as close friends.

Pet ownership in general can prove beneficial to humans. Unless your idea of a pet is a great white shark or disease-ridden bonobo, the animal will be there for you in sickness and in health. This is where cat and dog owners finally unite.

A UCLA study found that men with AIDS were, understandably, three times more likely to suffer from depression than men without the virus. But of those men suffering from AIDS, cat and dog owners were two times less likely to suffer from depression. A 1991 Australian study found that pet ownership helped reduce cholesterol and systolic blood pressure.

A 1980 study in *Public Health Report* found that the survival rate of people who have suffered heart attacks is much higher among pet owners. Of the 39 non-pet owners studied, one-quarter died within a year. Compare this with the death rate of pet owners, which was only six percent. When Dr. Erika Friedmann and colleagues first published this study, it was groundbreaking. Today, studies that monitor the recovery rate of patients suffering from other illnesses have proven the outcome to be repeatable and consistent.

A 1996 study in *Applied Animal Behavior Science* found pets to be great confidence boosters for teenagers, who, as we all know, need confidence the most. Of the 47 middle-school subjects studied, the teens who lived with pets were less fearful and had higher self-esteem. A 1991 article in *Children's Environments Quarterly* reported that kindergarten children with pets were less likely to have behavioral problems, according to their mothers and teachers.

These may be coincidences, but various studies have shown that early signs of animal cruelty perpetrated by children are higher in children that did not grow up with pets. And since animal cruelty is a big indicator of behavioral disturbance, and a reliable sign that a child may one day lean toward criminal activities, is it possible that having more cats in more children's settings could make the world a better place?

Maybe, or maybe they'll just end up as crazy cat people like you and me.

Notes on Sources

Anderson, Allen and Linda. *Angel Cats*. 1st ed. Toronto: New World Library, 2004.

"Animal Abuse Case Details: Cat stolen, dropped off 15 miles from home Fort Lauderdale, FL (US)." Pet-Abuse.com. 22 March 2005. http://www.petabuse.com/cases/4095/FL/US/

Bartel, Pauline. *Amazing Animal Actors*. Dallas: Taylor Publishing, 1997.

Brennen, Carlene Fredericka. *Hemingway's Cats: An Illustrated Biography*. Sarasota: Pineapple Press Inc., 2006.

Bryant, Doris. *The Care and Handling of Cats: A Manual for Modern Cat Owners*. Rev. ed., New York: Ives Washburn Inc., 1949.

Buckley, Bonnie. "Military Mascots." 2007. http://www.military-mascots.org/

Caro, T.M. "Predatory Behaviour in Domestic Cat Mother." *Behaviour*, Vol. 74, No. 1–2 (1980): 128–47.

Chesler, Phyllis. "Maternal Influence in Learning by Observation in Kittens." *Science*, Vol. 166, No. 3907 (1969): 901–03.

Christensen, Wendy. "The Clone Wars." *Cat Fancy*. June 2002: 41–43.

"Dewey Readmore Books." Spencer Library. January 2008. http://spencerlibrary.com/deweybio.htm

"Domestic Cat Genome Sequenced." Science Daily. 1 November 2007. http://www.sciencedaily.com/releases/2007/10/071031172826.htm

Dosa, M.D., and M.P.H. David. "A Day in the Life of Oscar the Cat." *New England Journal of Medicine*, Vol. 357, No. 4 (2007): 328–29.

Edney, Andrew T.B. "Companion Animals and Human Health: An Overview." *Journal of the Royal Society of Medicine*, Vol. 88, No. 12 (1995): 704–08.

Figueroa, Teri. "Trial Over Cat and Dog Fight Starts Today." *North County Times*. 26 January 2004. http://www.nctimes.com/articles/2004/01/27/news/top_stories/1_26_0421_20_53.txt

Fitzpatrick, Sonya. *Cat Talk: The Secrets of Communicating with Your Cat*. 2nd ed. New York: Berkley Books, 2004.

Friedmann, Erika, Aaron Honori Katcher, James J. Lynch, and Sue Ann Thomas. "Animal Companions and One-Year Survival of Patients After Discharge from a Coronary Care Unit." *Public Health Reports*, Vol. 95, No. 4 (1980): 307–12.

Furst, Gennifer. "Prison-Based Animal Programs: A National Survey." *The Prison Journal*, 86, No. 4 (2006): 407–30.

Gallegos, Chris. "Cats in the Crossfire." *Cat Fancy*. December 2004.

Giammarino, Marie. Cats Info. 2001. 30 January 2008. http://www.catsinfo.com

Hall, John. "Mother Cat Takes on Extra Litter; Puppies Abandoned by Mother Adopted by Cat." *North County Times*. 27 April 2007. http://www.nctimes.com/articles/2007/04/27/news/californian/4_04_0720_55_48.txt

Holmes, Ronald. *Witchcraft in History.* 1st ed. Secaucus: Carol Publishing Group, 1977.

Johnson, Bridget. "War: Felines Show Amazing Resilience Under Fire." *Cat Fancy.* May 2003. 43–46.

Jay, Roni. *The Kingdom of the Cat.* 1st ed. London: Apple Press, 2000.

Jutras, Lisan. "Inmates Are Going to the Dogs—and Loving it." *Globe and Mail.* 9 October 2007. http://www.theglobeandmail.com/servlet/story/RTGAM.20071009.wlpetting09/BNStory/lifeMain/home

Lawrence, John. *The Cat from Hue: A Vietnam War Story.* 1st ed. New York: Public Affairs. 2002.

"Man Says Cat Called 911." CBS News. 2 January 2005. CBS Interactive Inc. 31 March 2008. http://www.cbsnews.com/stories/2006/01/02/national/main1172573.shtml

Millward, David. "Humphrey...the Downing Street Dossier." *Daily Telegraph.* 15 March 2005. http://www.telegraph.co.uk/news/main.jhtml?xml=/news/2005/03/14/ndoss14.xml

Nef, Nadine, MA. "The Cat Programme: An Animal-Assisted Therapy at Saxierriet Prison for Men." *Delta Society.* 6 October 2004. 30 January 2008. http://www.deltasociety.org/download/CorrectionalFacilities2.pdf

"New Breed Cats." November 1, 2007. http://newbreedcats.com/index.php

Novella, Steven. "Seizure Dogs and Death Cats." [Weblog NeuroLogica] 1 August 2007. New England Skeptical Society. http://www.theness.com/neurologicablog/index.php?p=72At

Patterson, Dr. Francine. *Koko's Kitten.* 1st ed. New York: Scholastic Press, 1987.

Roberts, Patrick. Purr-n-Fur. December 2007. http://www.purr-n-fur.org.uk/

Roma, Gary. "Library Cats Map." Iron Frog Productions. 21 September 2007. 1 January 2008. http://www.ironfrog.com/catsmap.html

Roosevelt, Theodore. "Theodore Roosevelt's Letters to His Children." New York: Charles Scribner's Sons, 1919. 1998. www.bartleby.com/53/

Rutherford, Alice Philomena (ed.). *The Readers Digest Illustrated Book of Cats.* Montreal: The Readers Digest Association (Canada) Ltd., 1992.

Seitz, Philip FD, MDA. "Infantile Experience and Adult Behavior in Animal Subjects." *Psychosomatic Medicine,* 21 (1959): 353–78.

Singer, Marilyn. *Cats to the Rescue.* 1st ed. New York: Henry Holt and Company, 2006.

Strand, Elizabeth B. "Interparental Conflict and Youth Maladjustment: The Buffering Effects of Pets." *Stress, Trauma, and Crisis,* 7 (2004): 151–68.

Turner, Dennis C., and Paul Patrick. *The Domestic Cat: The Biology of its Behaviour.* 2nd ed. Cambridge: Cambridge University Press, 2000.

"What Kills Birds?" Curry & Kerlinger, LLC. 5 January 2008. http://www.currykerlinger.com/birds.htm

Omar Mouallem

Small-town resident turned urbanite Omar
Mouallem has been published internationally,
and his articles, movie reviews and short stories
have been seen across Canada, in England and
the Middle East. Omar is also a hip-hop artist
who performs under the moniker "A.O.K."
(www.assaultofknowledge.com).

With his satirical and droll writing style, Omar,
a bona fide cat lover, sees the humor in the fact
that cats hated him. Throughout the years, all but
two of his cats have run away, proving, for Omar,
that his cats really don't come back, no matter
what the song says.

Here are more titles from
FOLKLORE PUBLISHING...

AMAZING DOGS
Stories of Brilliance, Loyalty, Courage & Extraordinary Feats
by Lisa Wojna

From Stubby, the mongrel mutt whose barking saved sleeping
soldiers from poisonous gas during World War I, to Dodger, the
beagle who was rescued after a mama bear claimed him as her
cub, these dogs have done it all!

$18.95 • ISBN10: 1-894864-72-7 • ISBN13: 978-1-894864-72-5
• 5.25" x 8.25" • 272 pages

Canadarm and the accomplishments of a͟s͟t͟r͟o͟ ͟ ͟ ͟ ͟uch ͟a͟s Marc
Garneau, Roberta Bondar and Chris Hatfield, read about the
amazing contributions Canada has made to space research and
discovery.

$18.95 • ISBN10: 1-894864-59-X • ISBN13: 978-1-894864-59-6
• 5.25" x 8.25" • 264 pages

REAL CANADIAN PIRATES
Buccaneers & Rogues of the North
by Geordie Telfer

Yes, there really were Canadian pirates, and they didn't always
say "please," "thank you" and "excuse me," either. Discover
the stories of Peter Easton, Bartholomew "Black Bart" Roberts,
Simeon Perkins, Bill Johnston, the Liverpool Packet and more.

$18.95 • ISBN10: 1-894864-70-0 • ISBN13: 978-1-894864-70-1
• 5.25" x 8.25" • 264 pages